the end, the beginning

a sisyphean cycle

widarto adi

Layout:
@dartodesign

To purchase or license images/prints please contact:
dartophoto@gmail.com

ISBN-13: 978-1530098507

ISBN-10: 1530098505

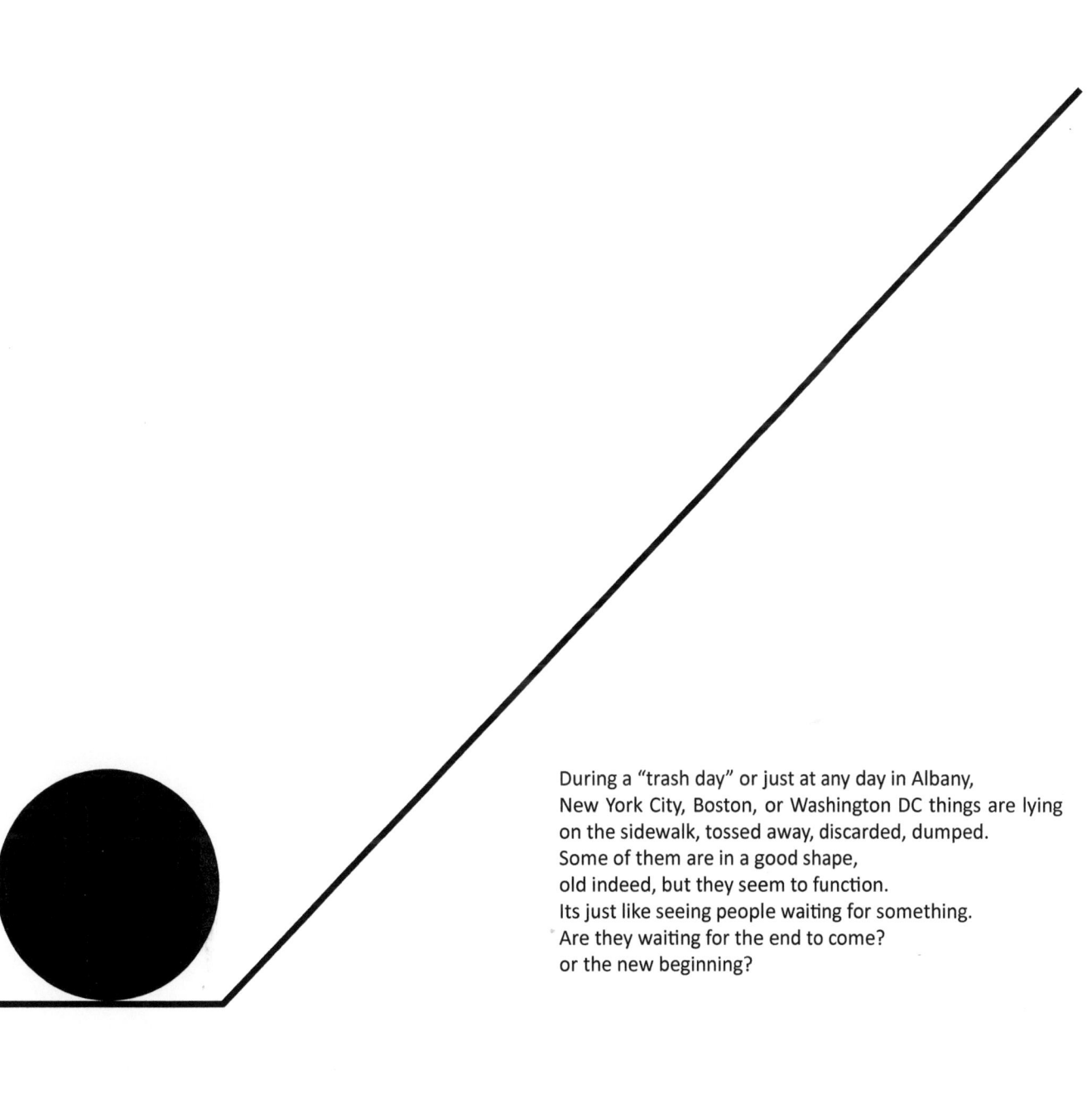

During a "trash day" or just at any day in Albany,
New York City, Boston, or Washington DC things are lying
on the sidewalk, tossed away, discarded, dumped.
Some of them are in a good shape,
old indeed, but they seem to function.
Its just like seeing people waiting for something.
Are they waiting for the end to come?
or the new beginning?

"In three words I can sum up everything I've learned about life: it goes on."
- Robert Frost

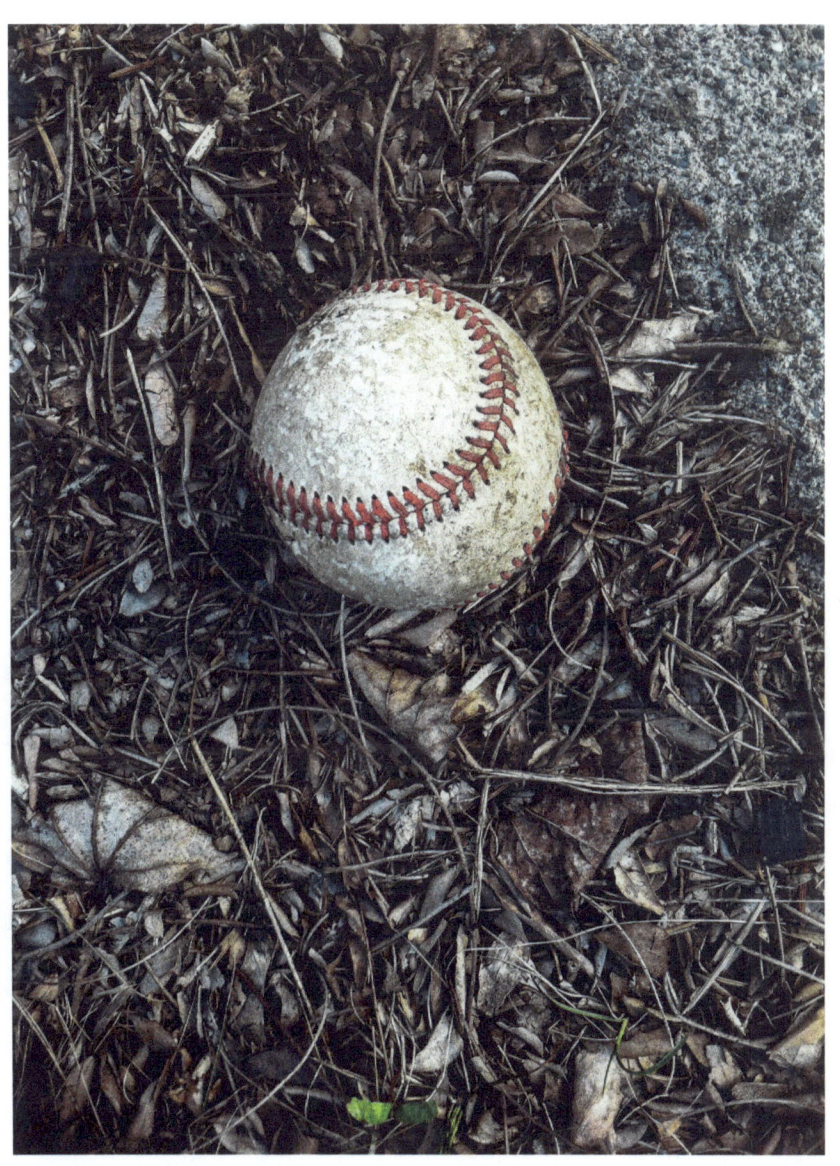

5

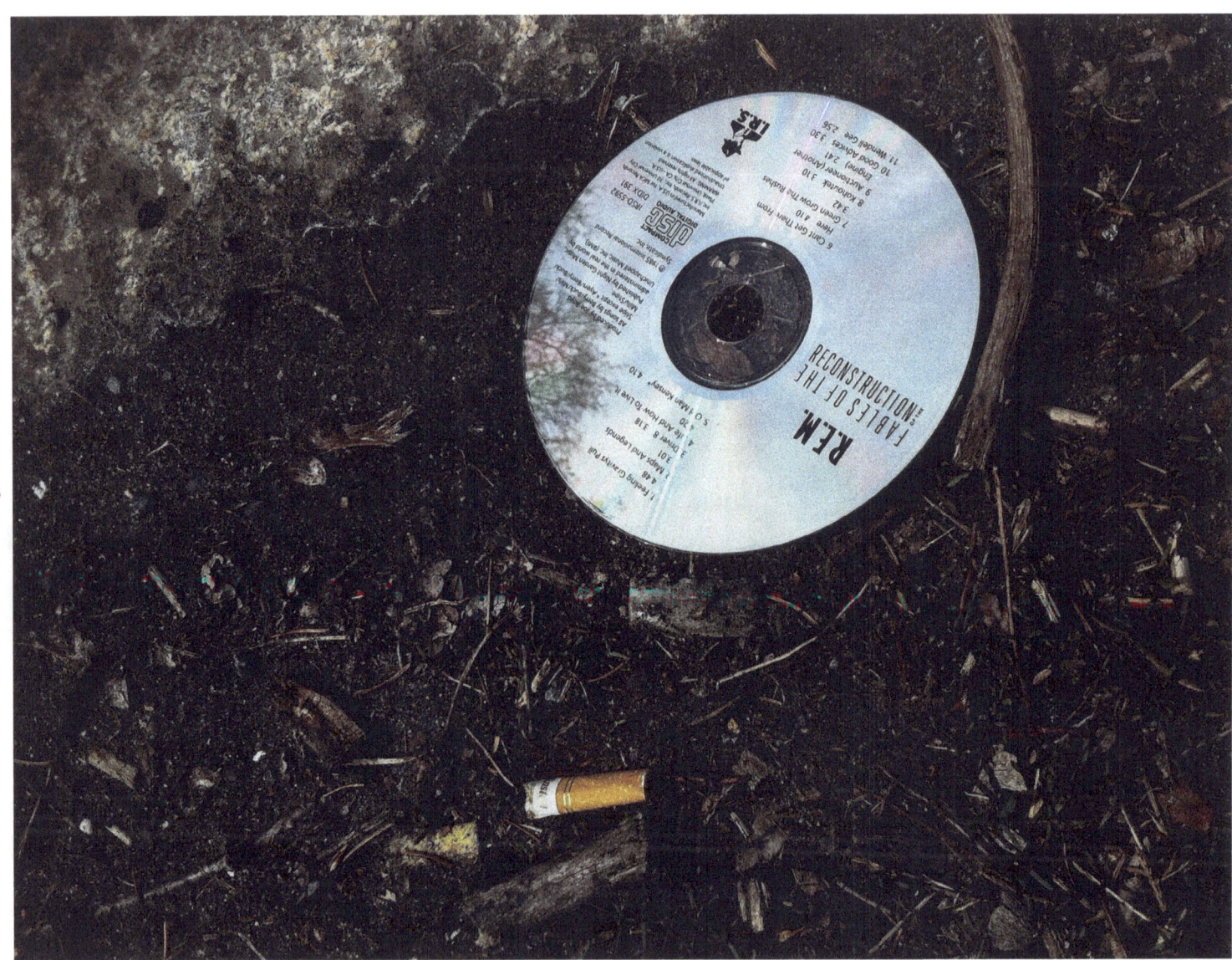

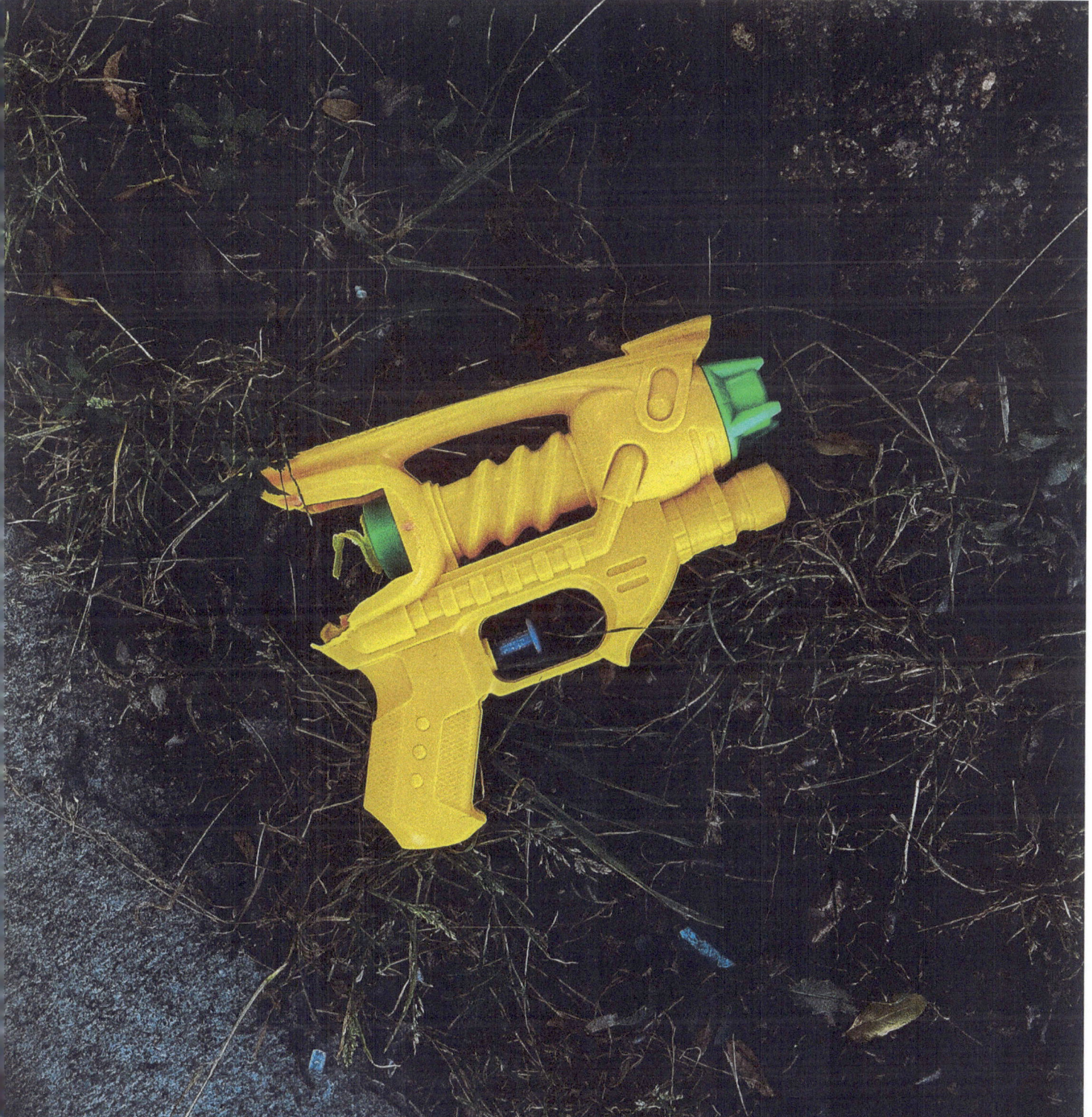

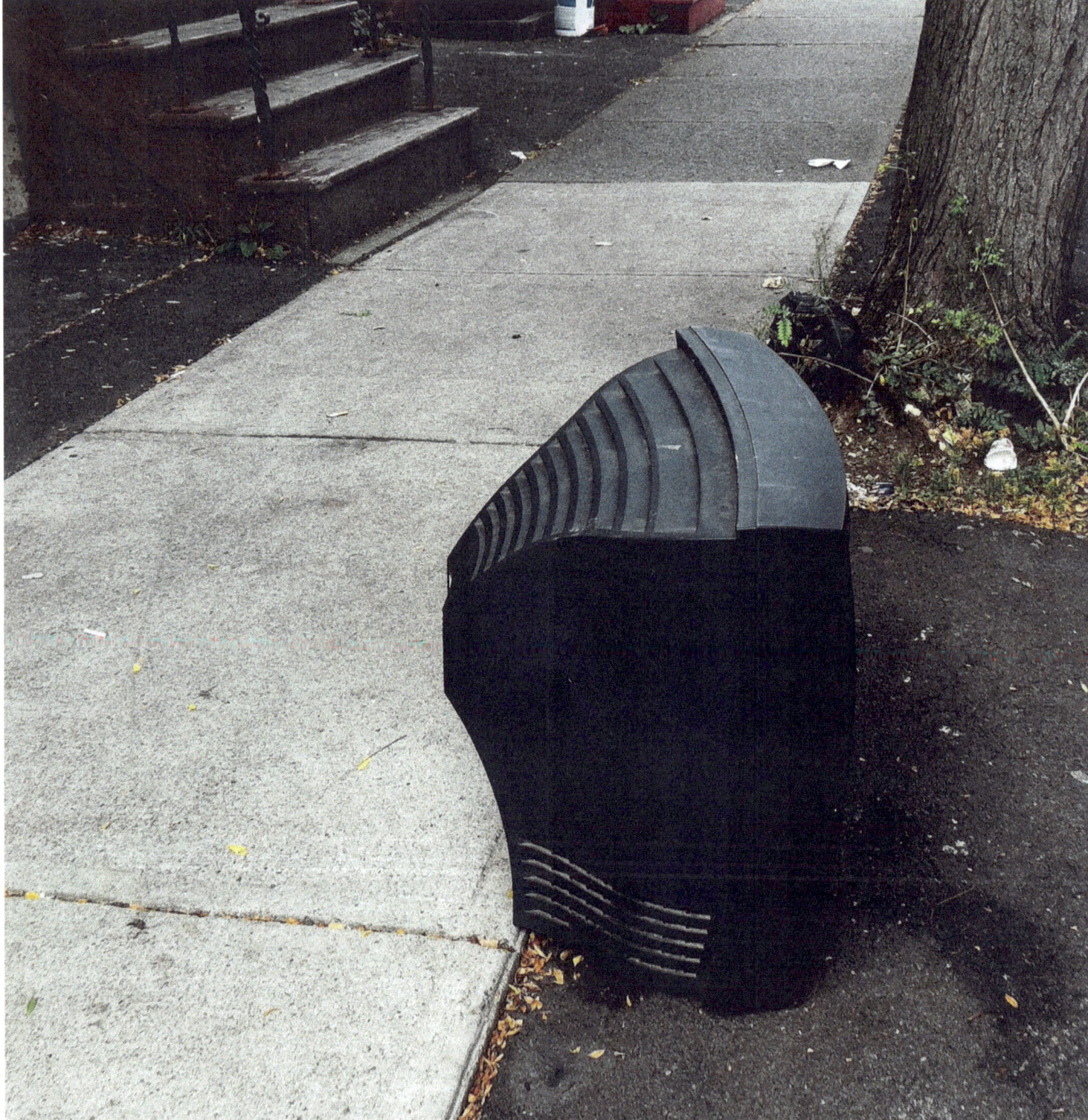

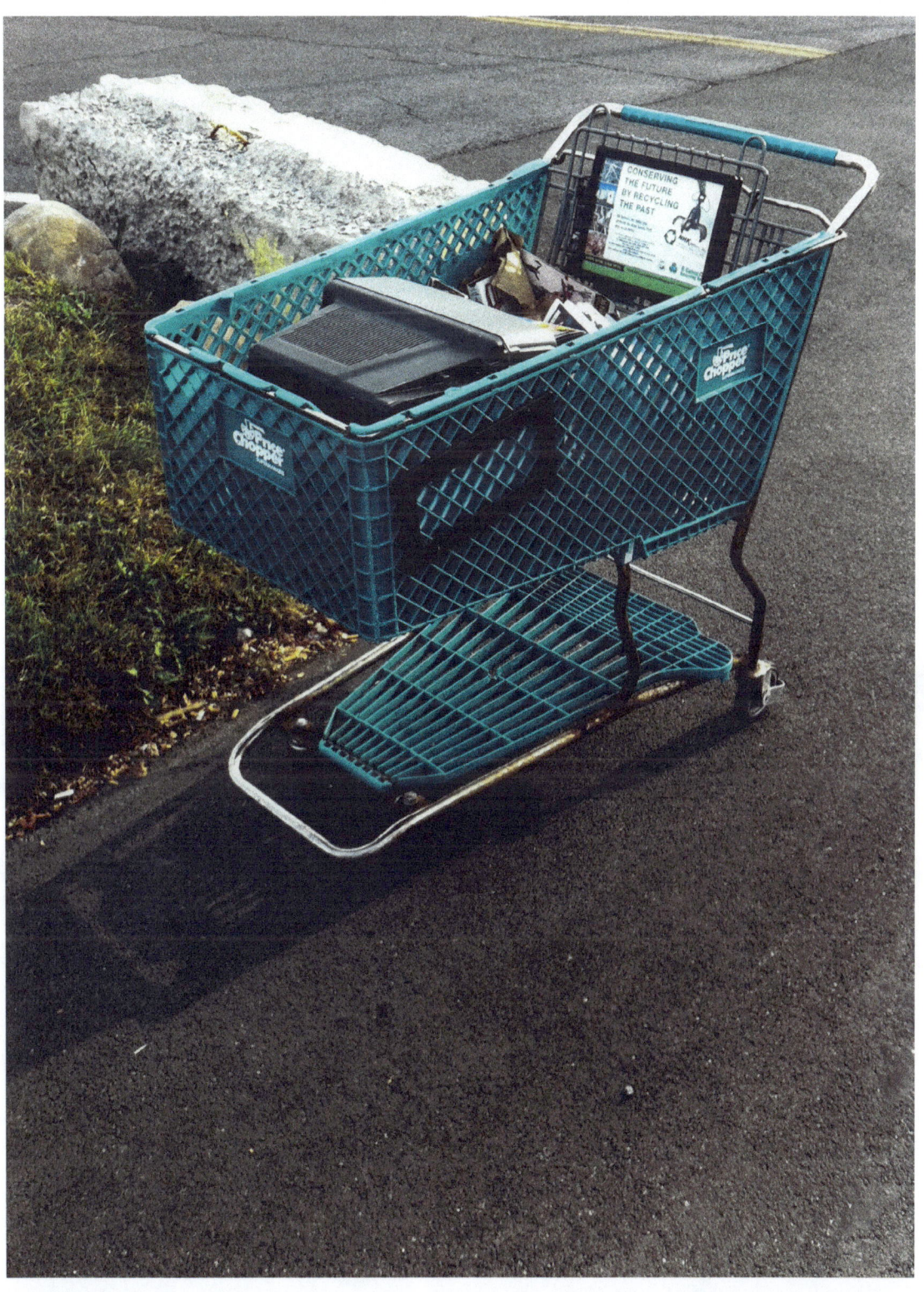

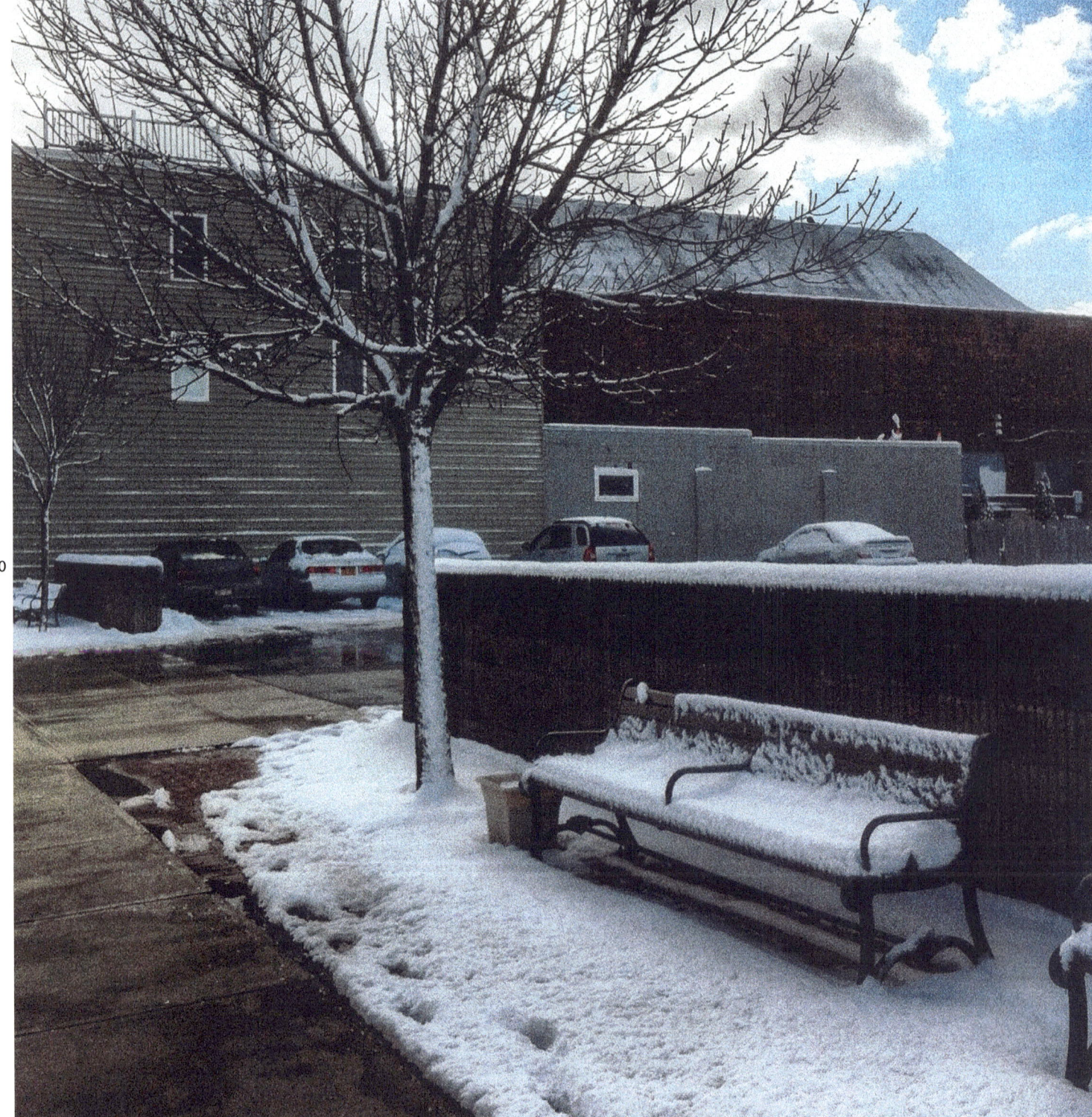

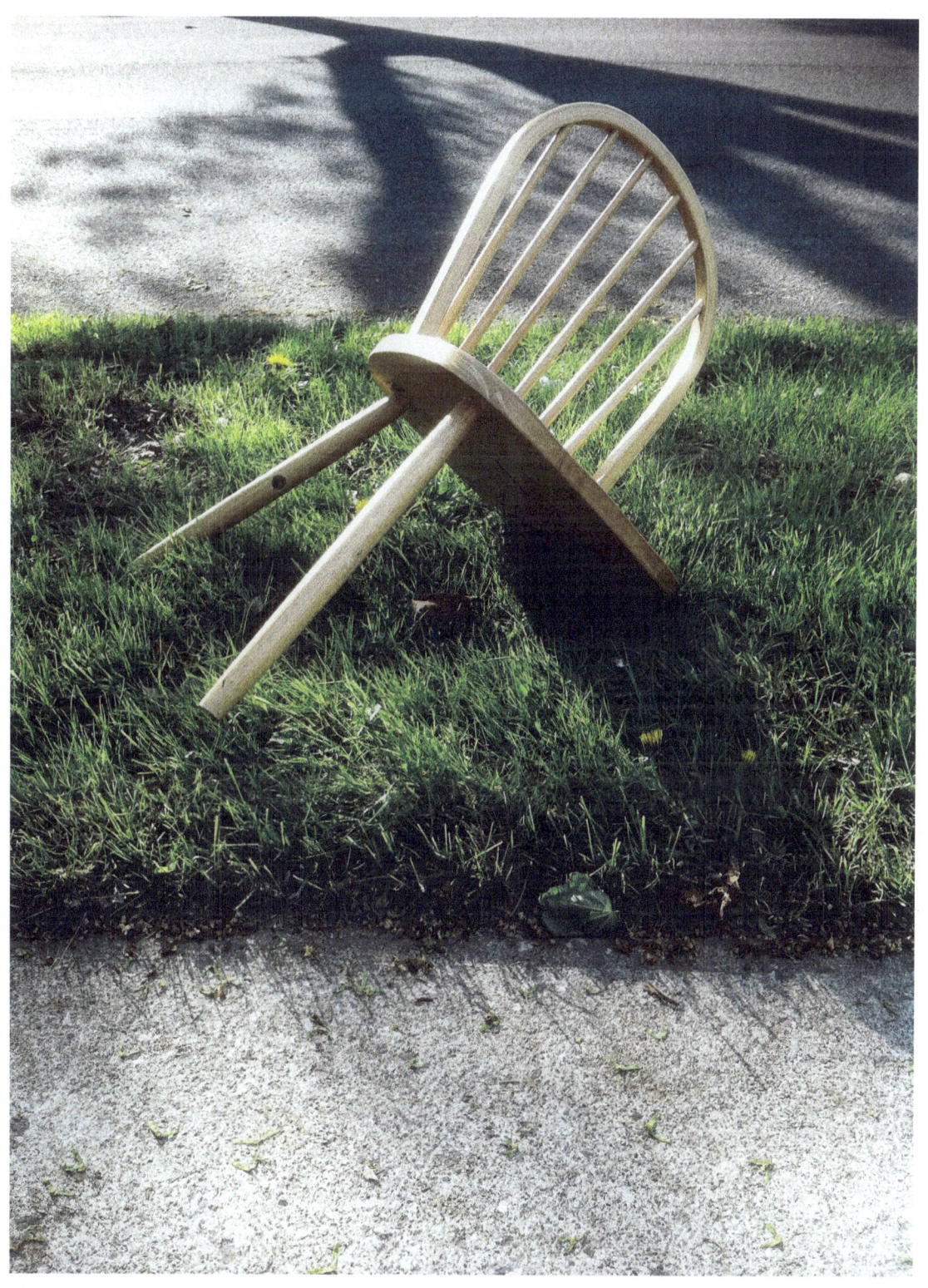

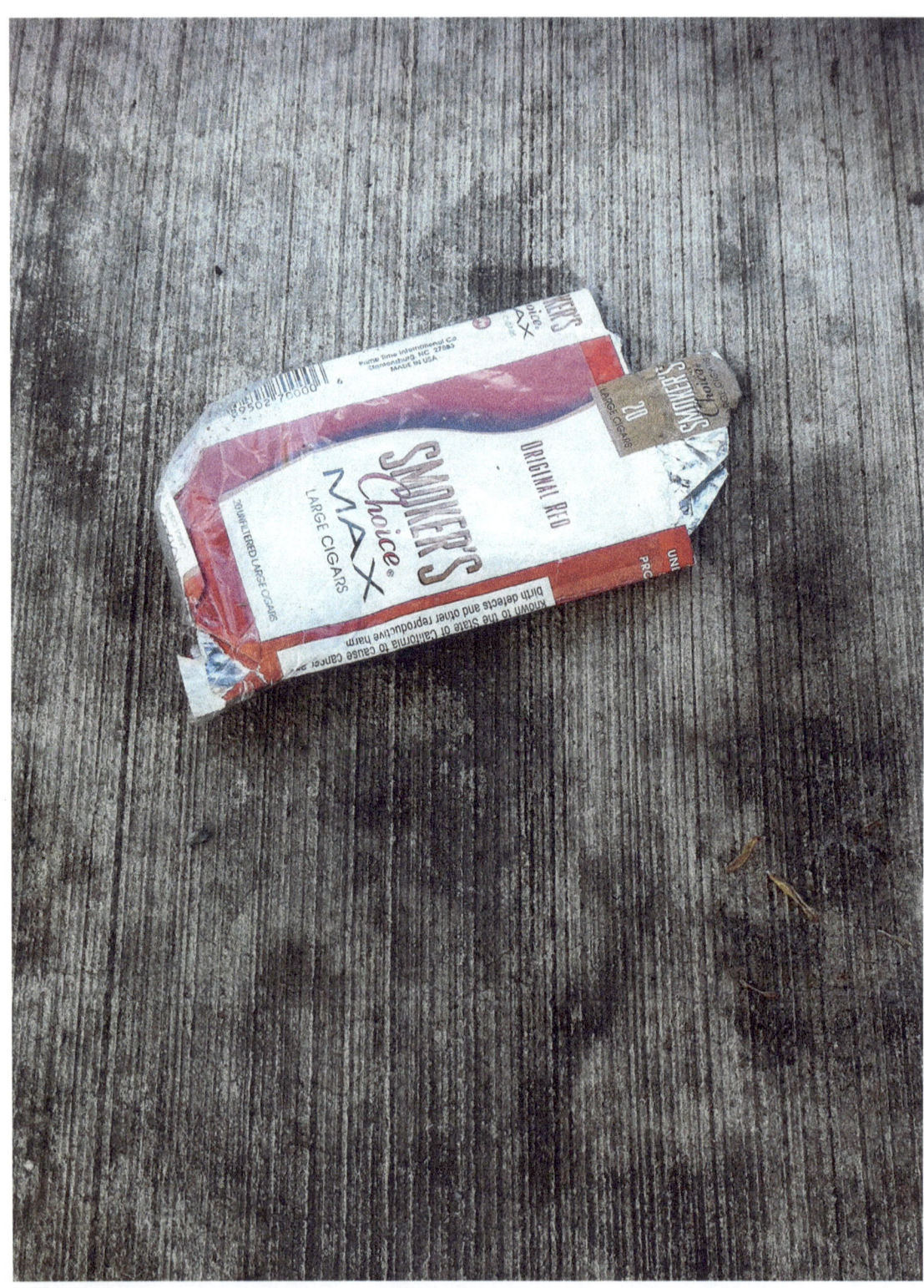

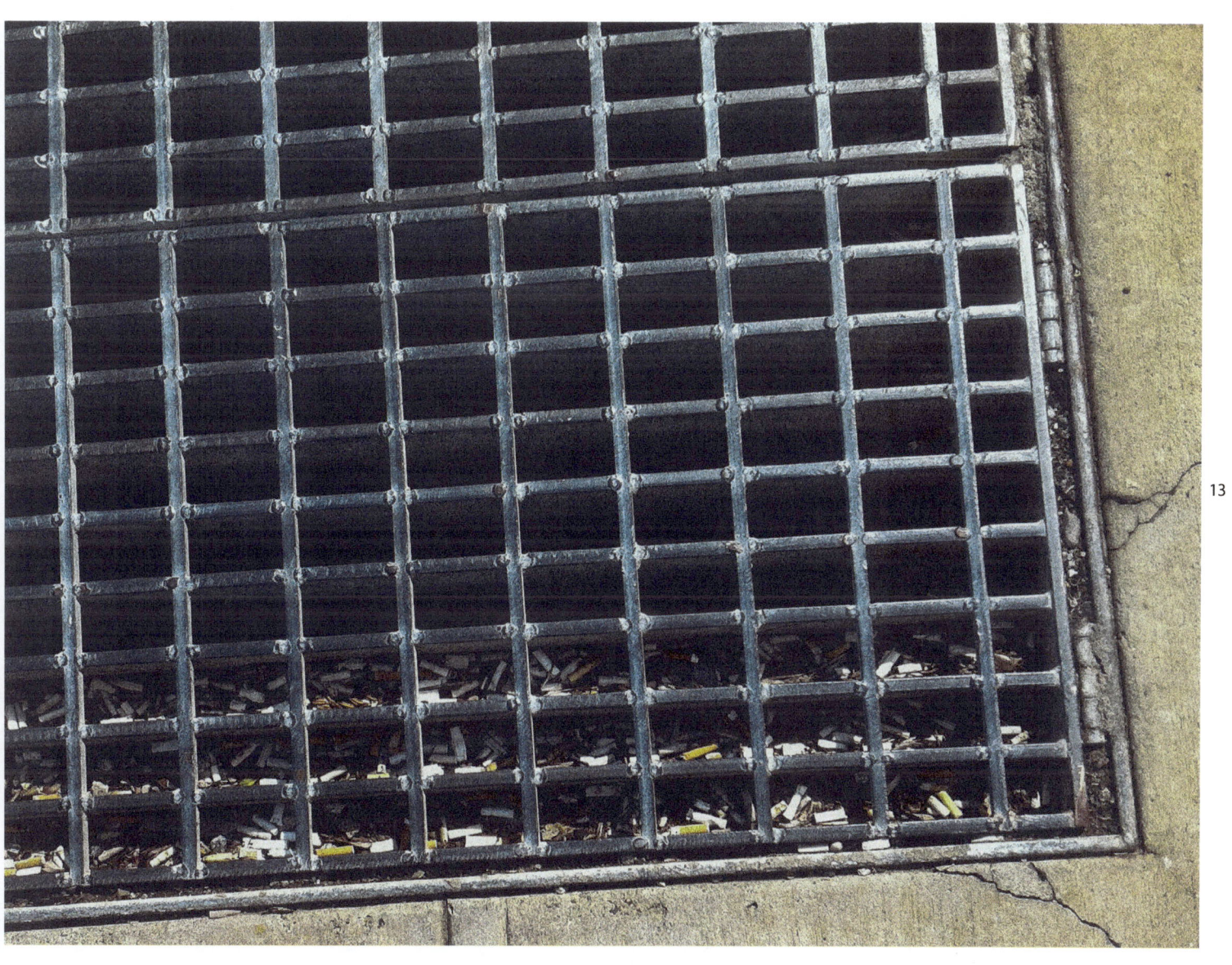

14

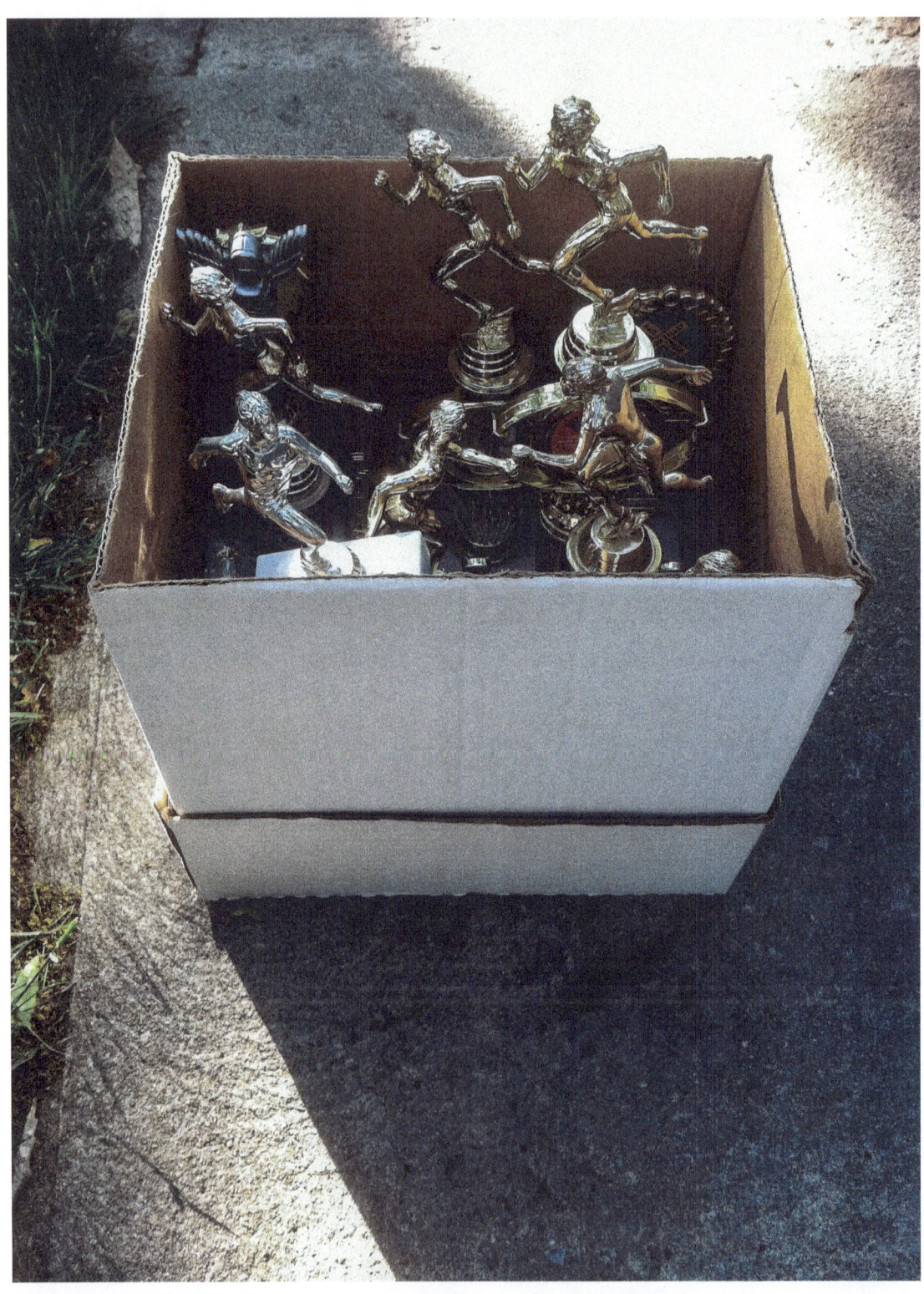

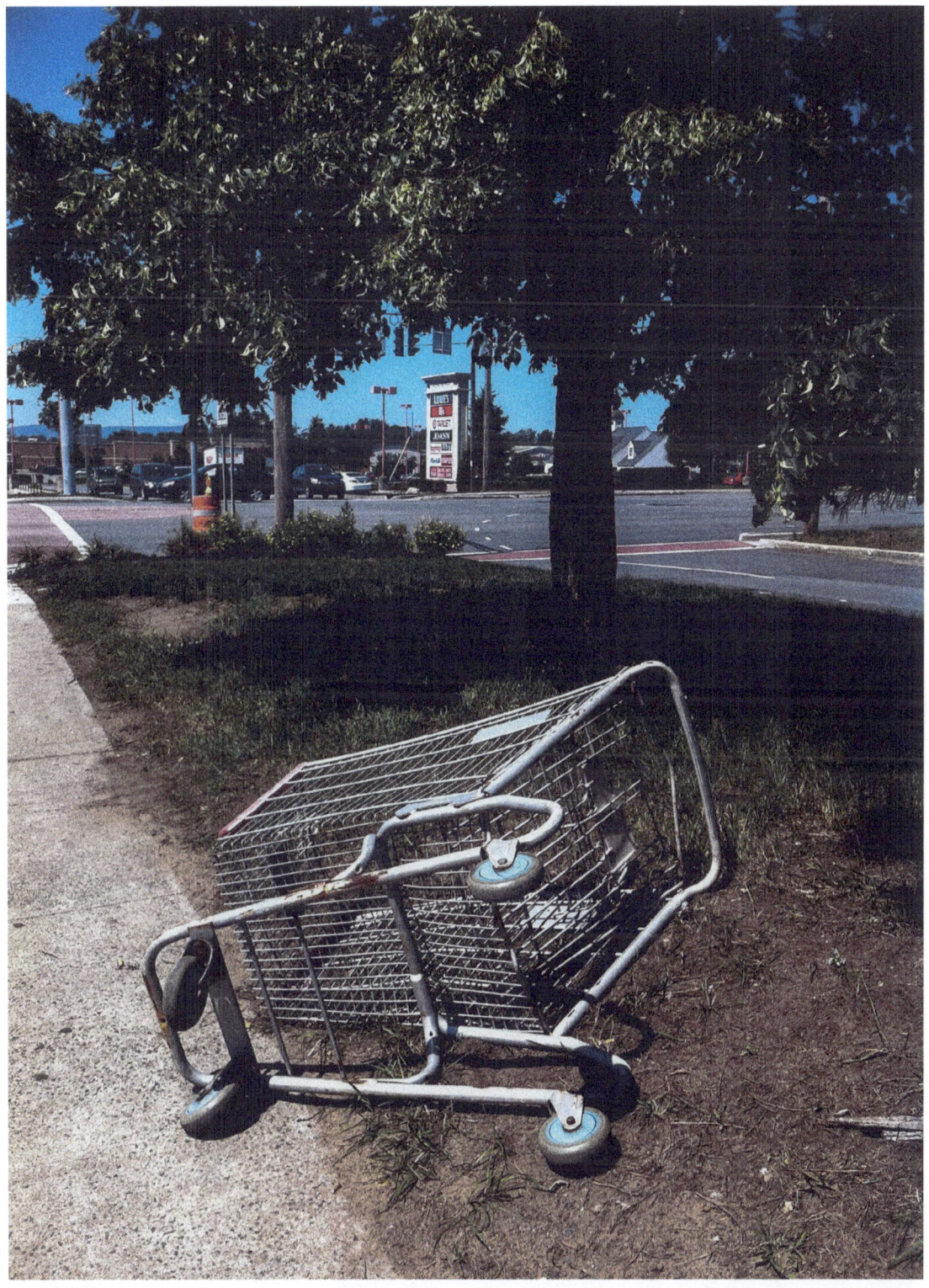

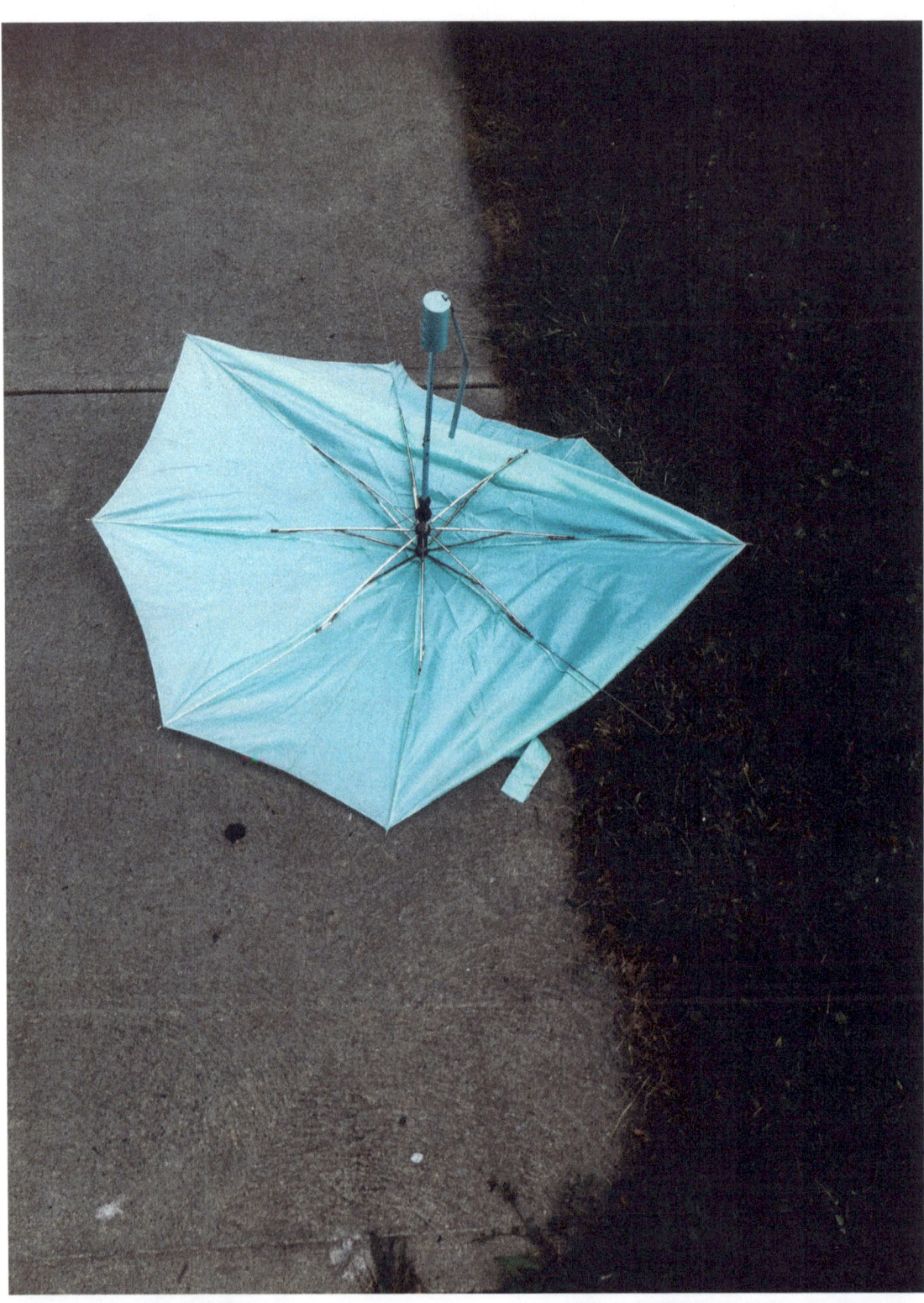

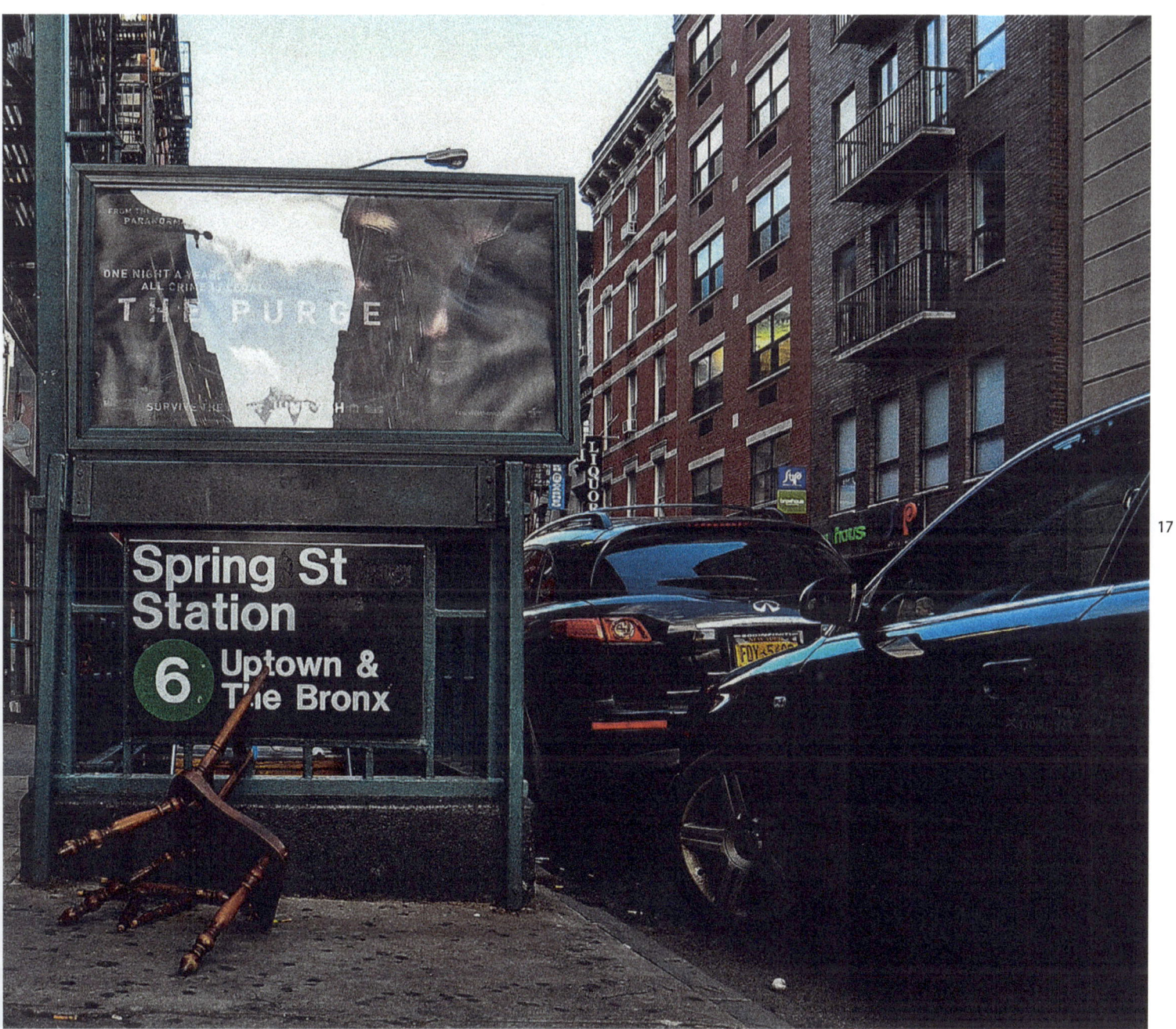

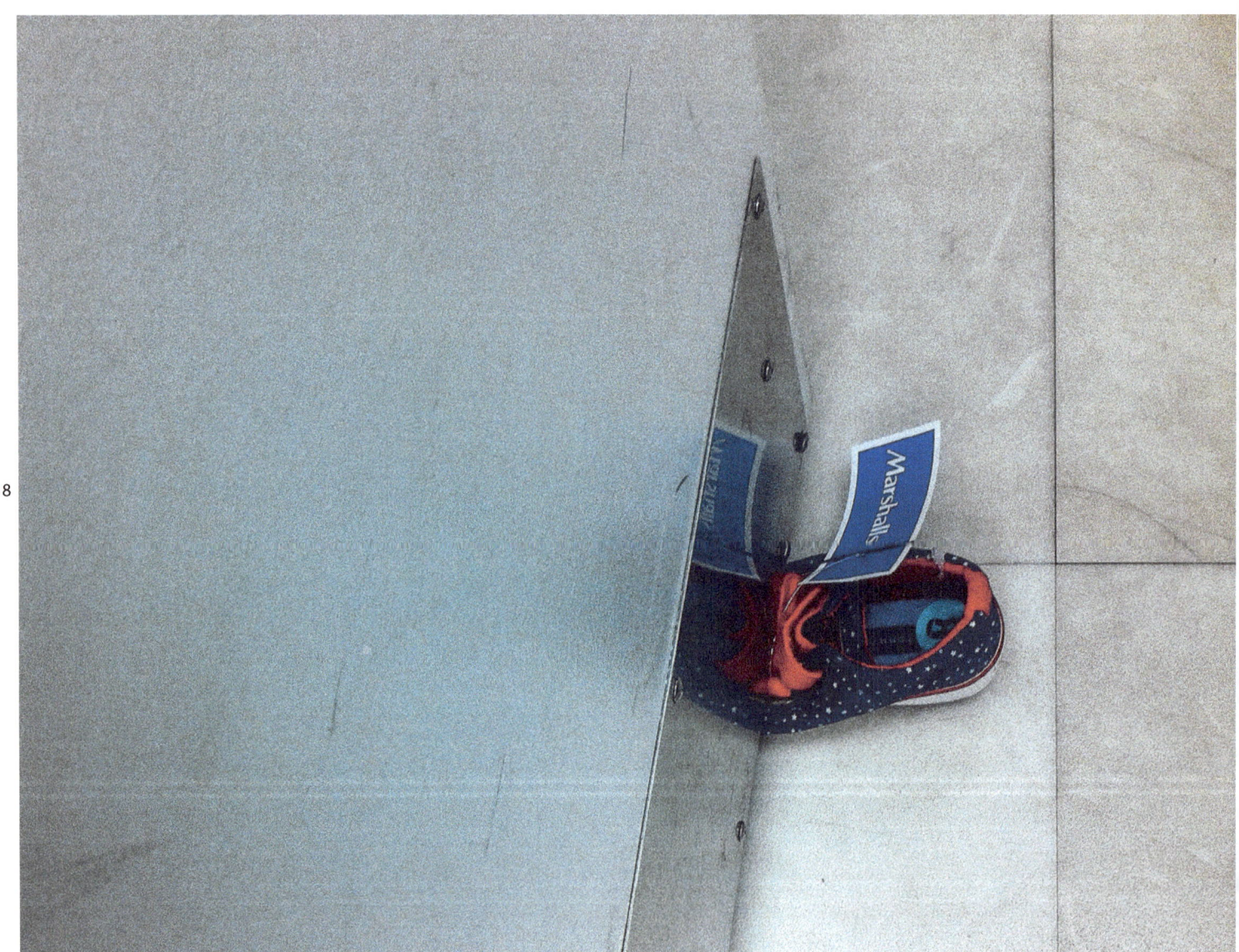

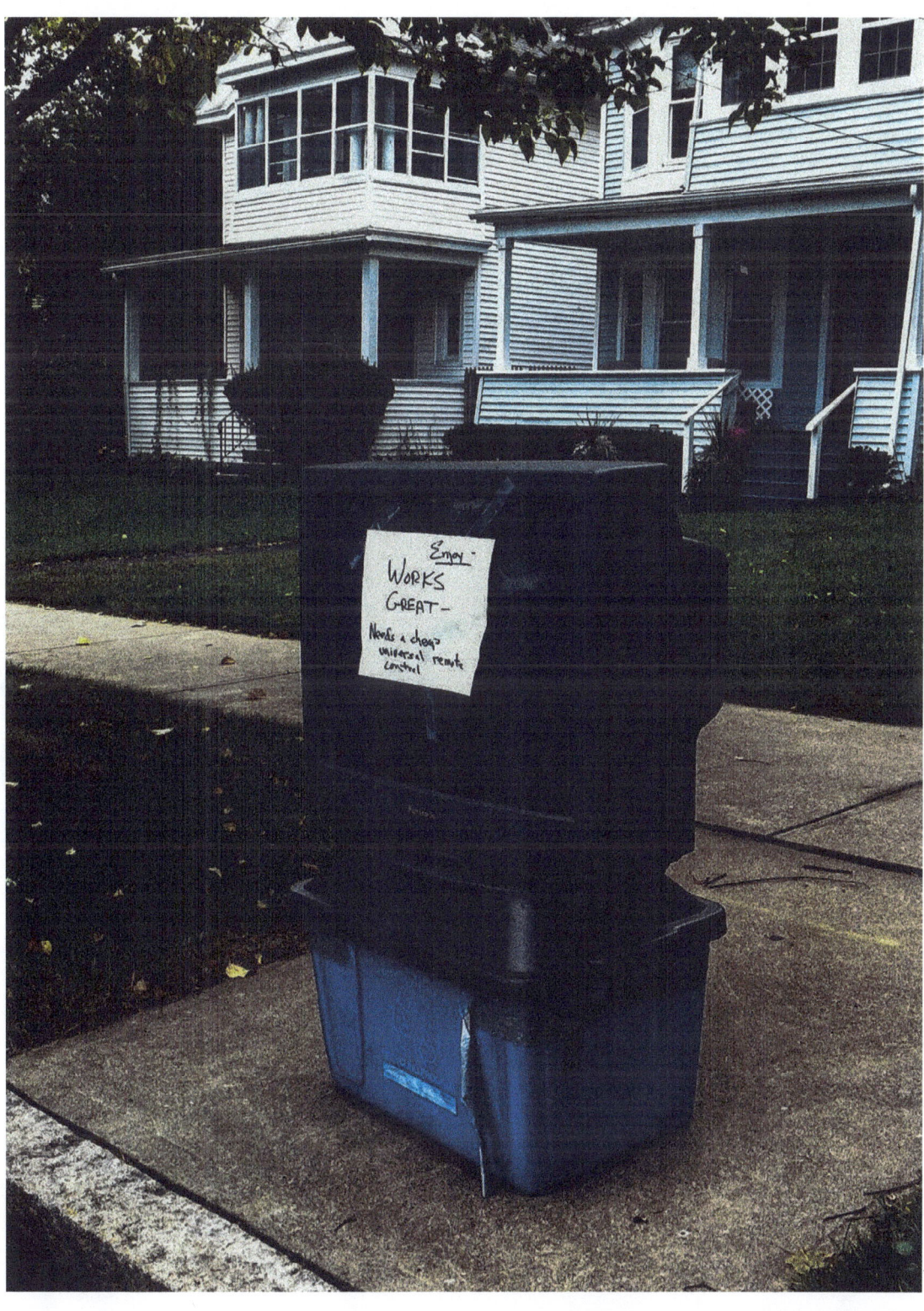

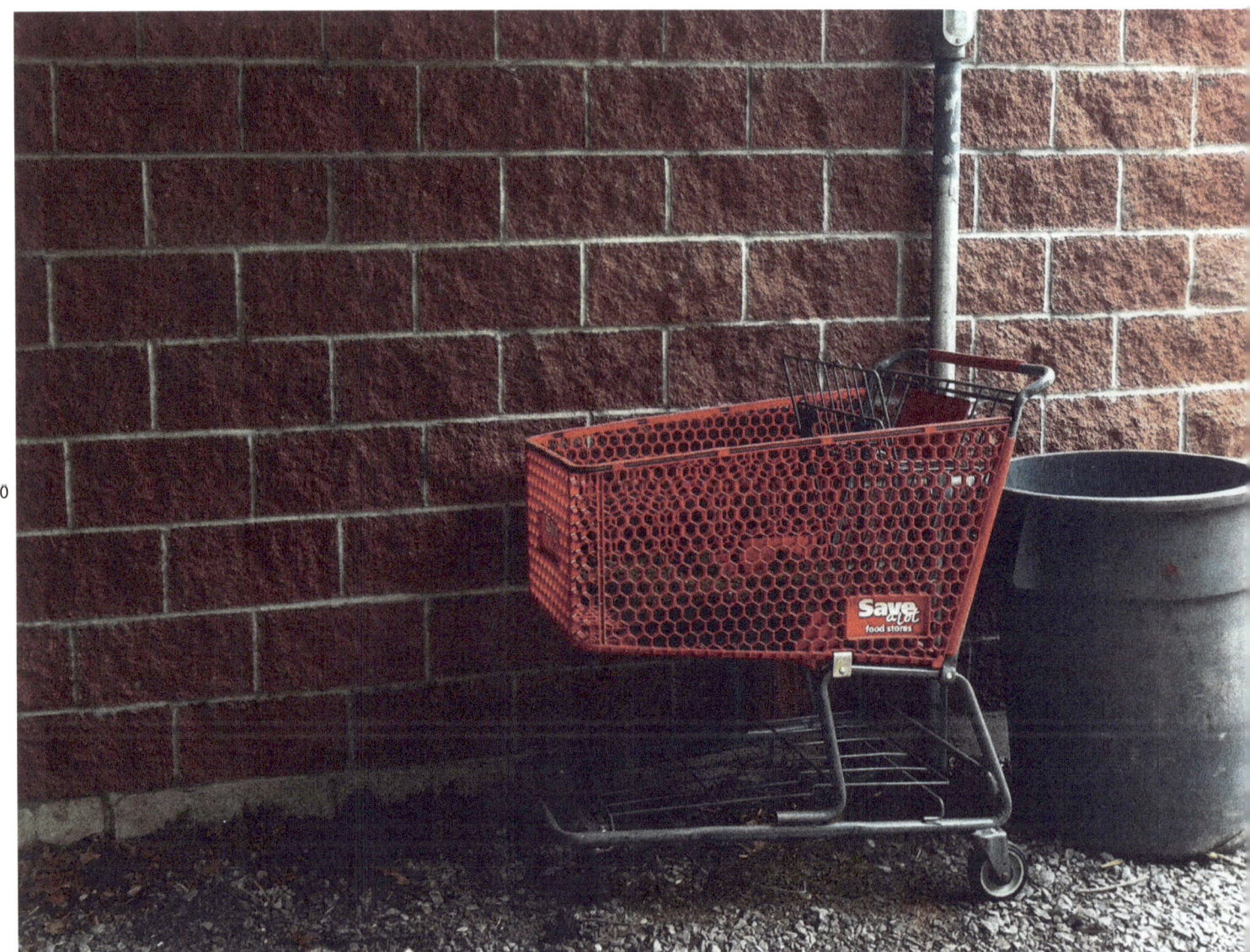

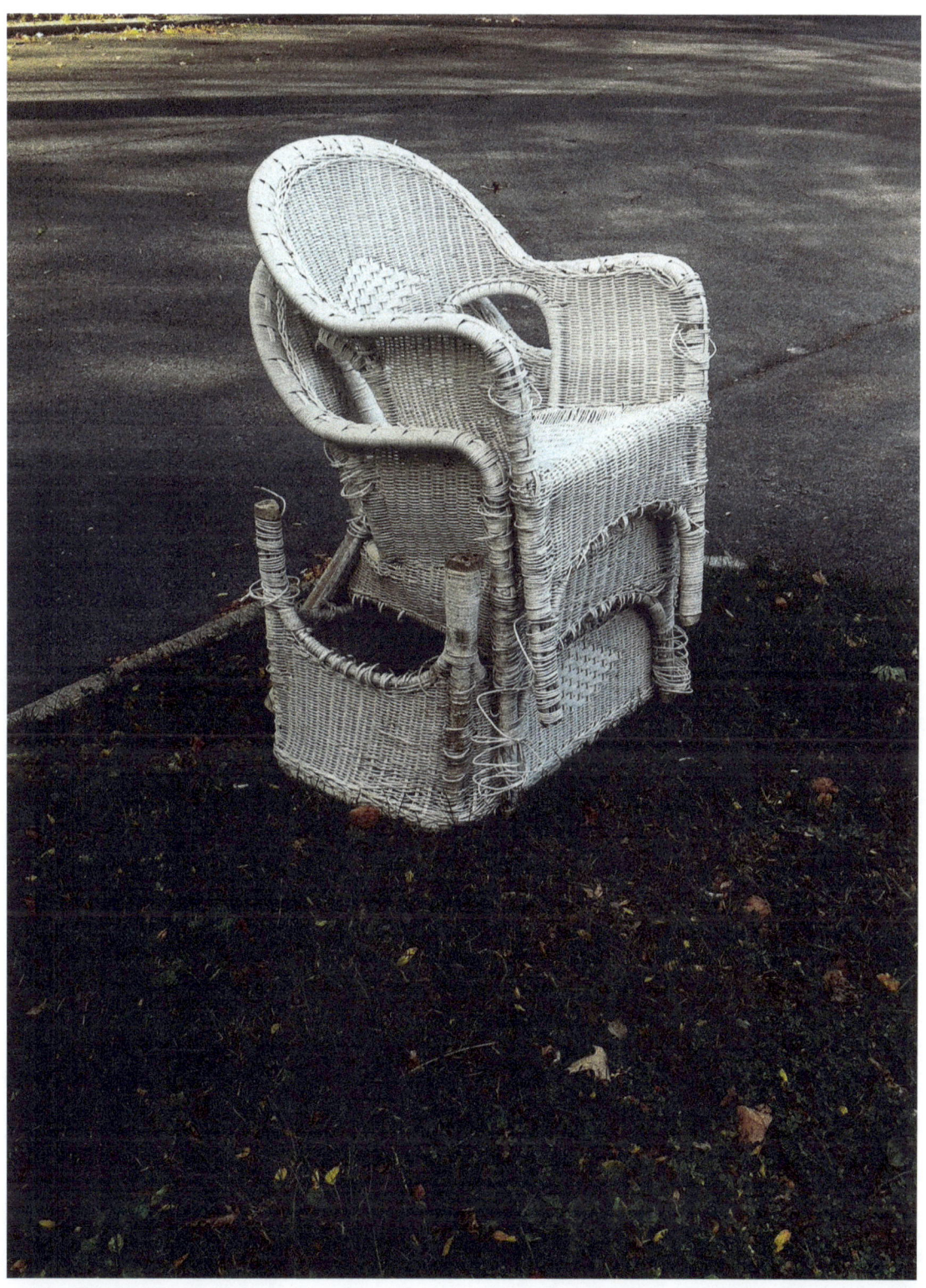

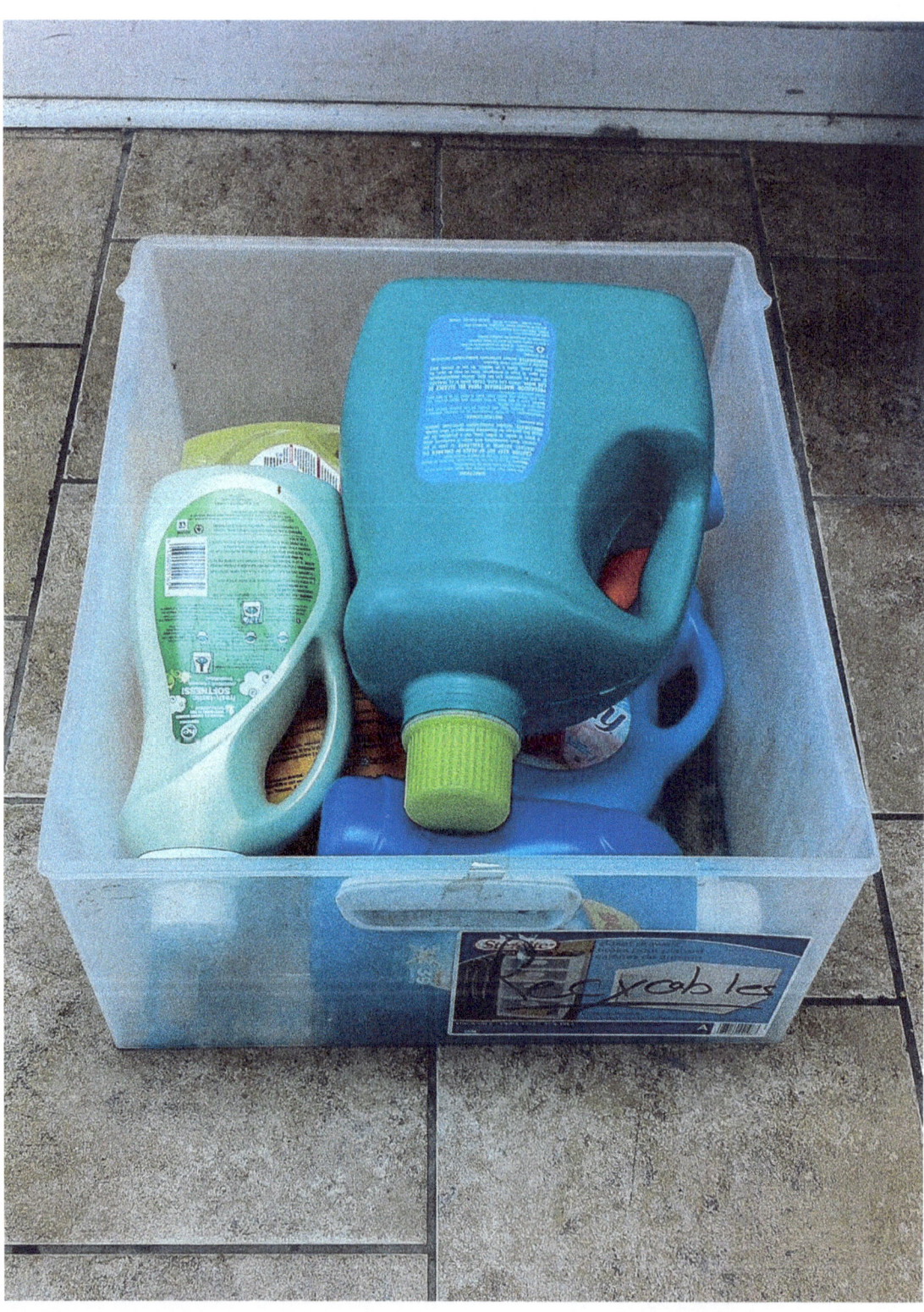

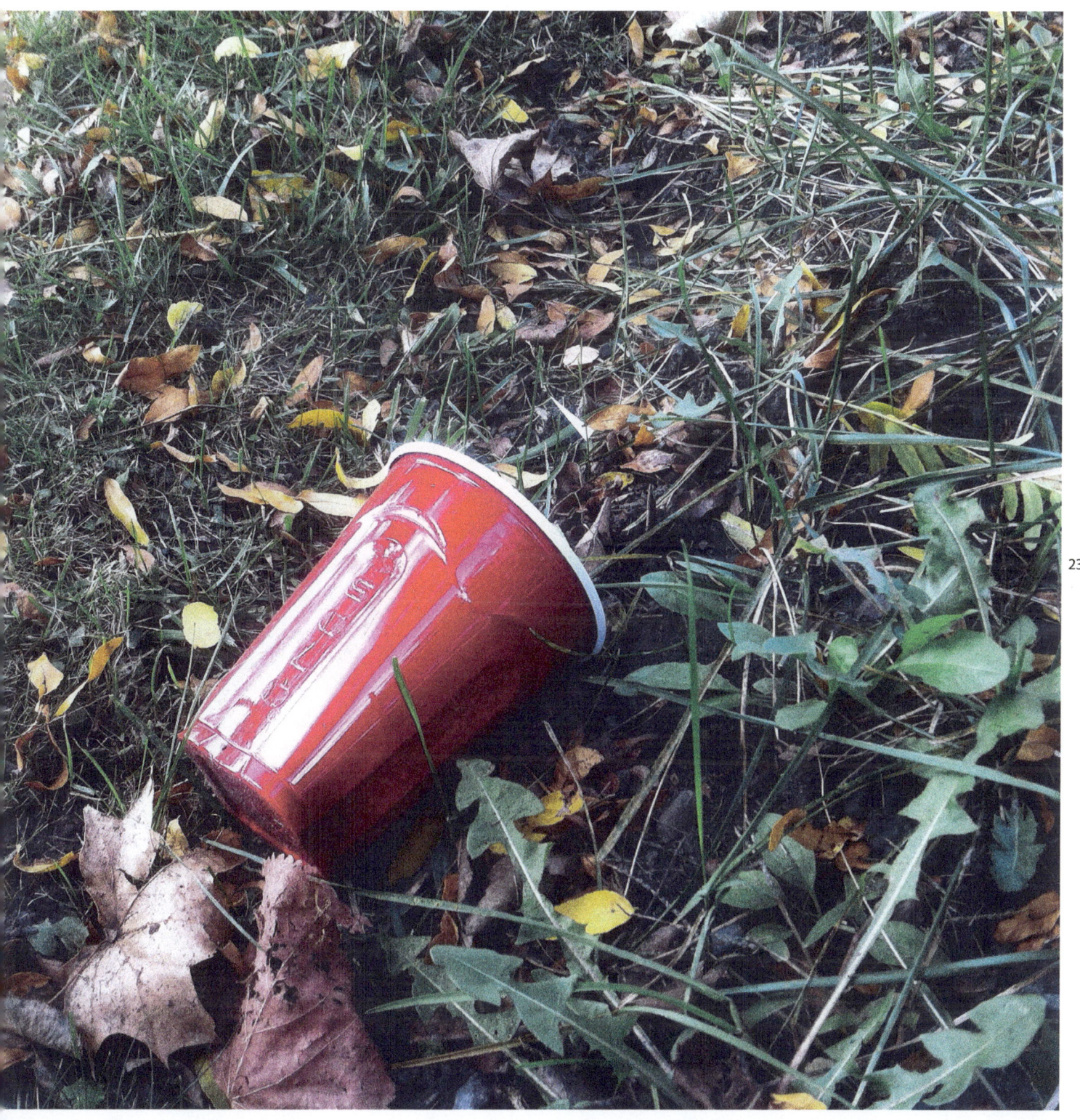

24

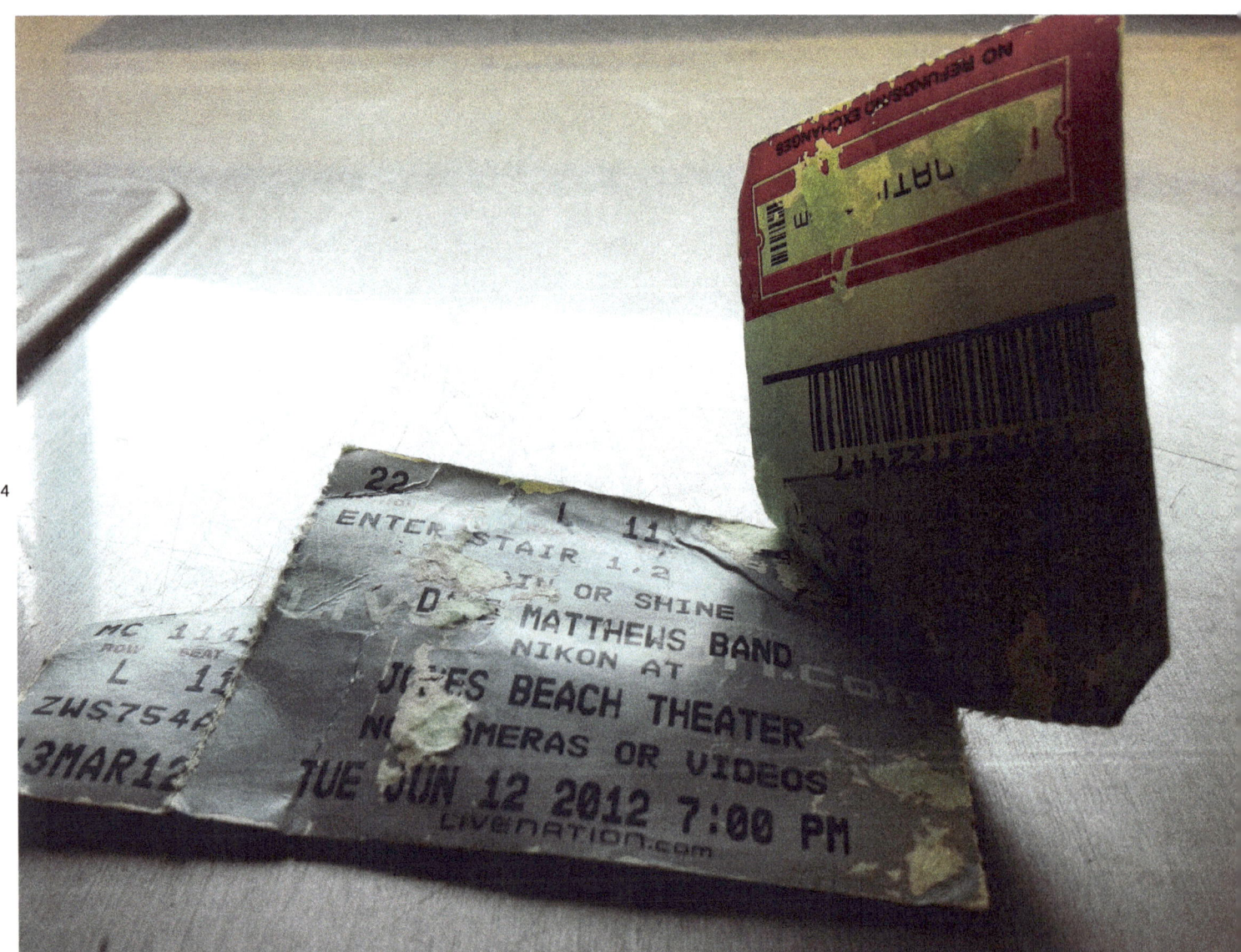

Good Luck × 3

The next day, three things happened to Judy. Three good-luck things.

Judy woke up just like she did on any other normal old day. She ran downstairs to eat breakfast just like she did on any other normal old day.

"Stink, pass the Lucky Os, please."

Stink passed the cereal. Judy poured Lucky Os into her bowl. She added milk.

That's when it happened. Good-Luck Thing Number One.

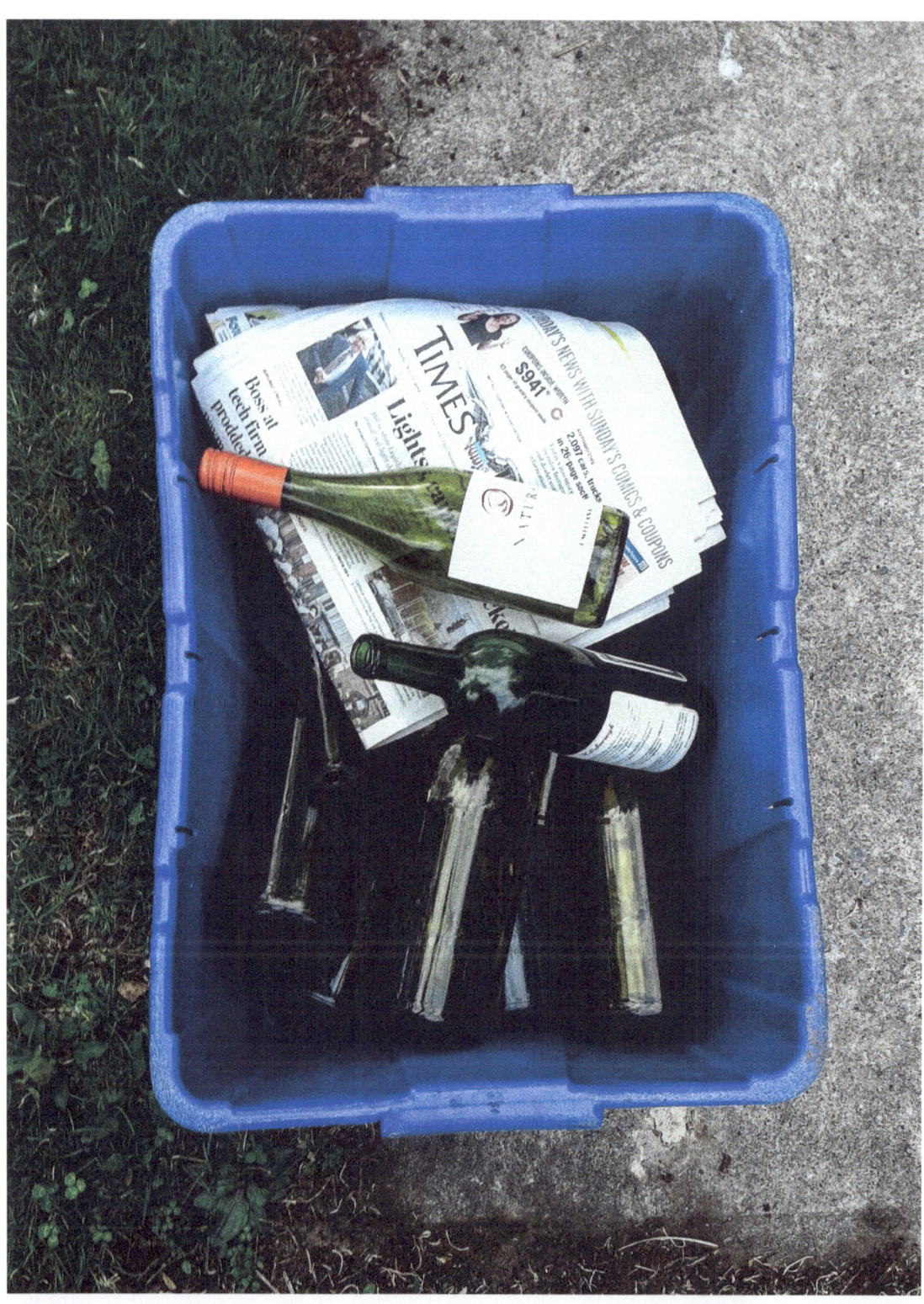

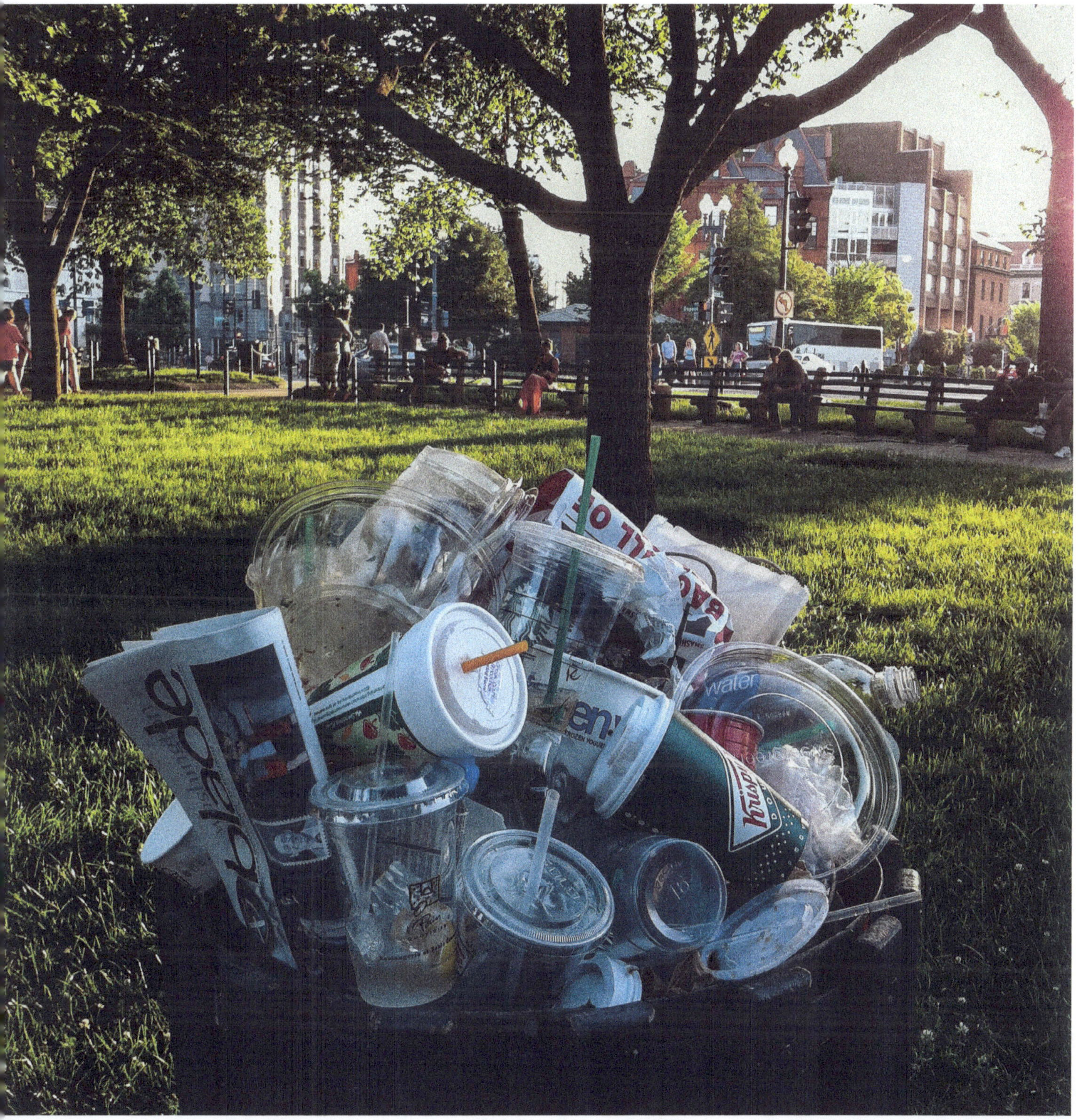

27

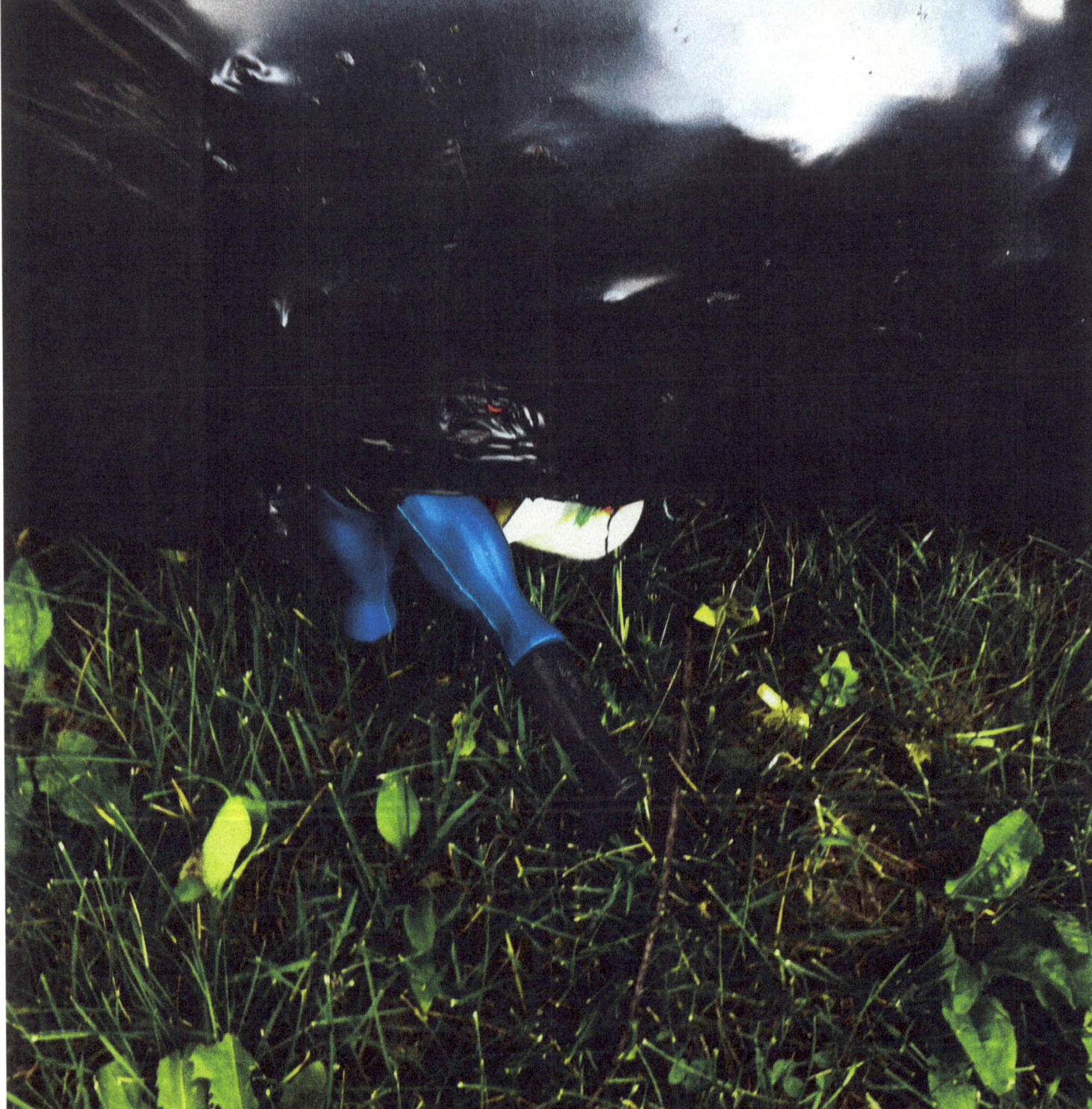

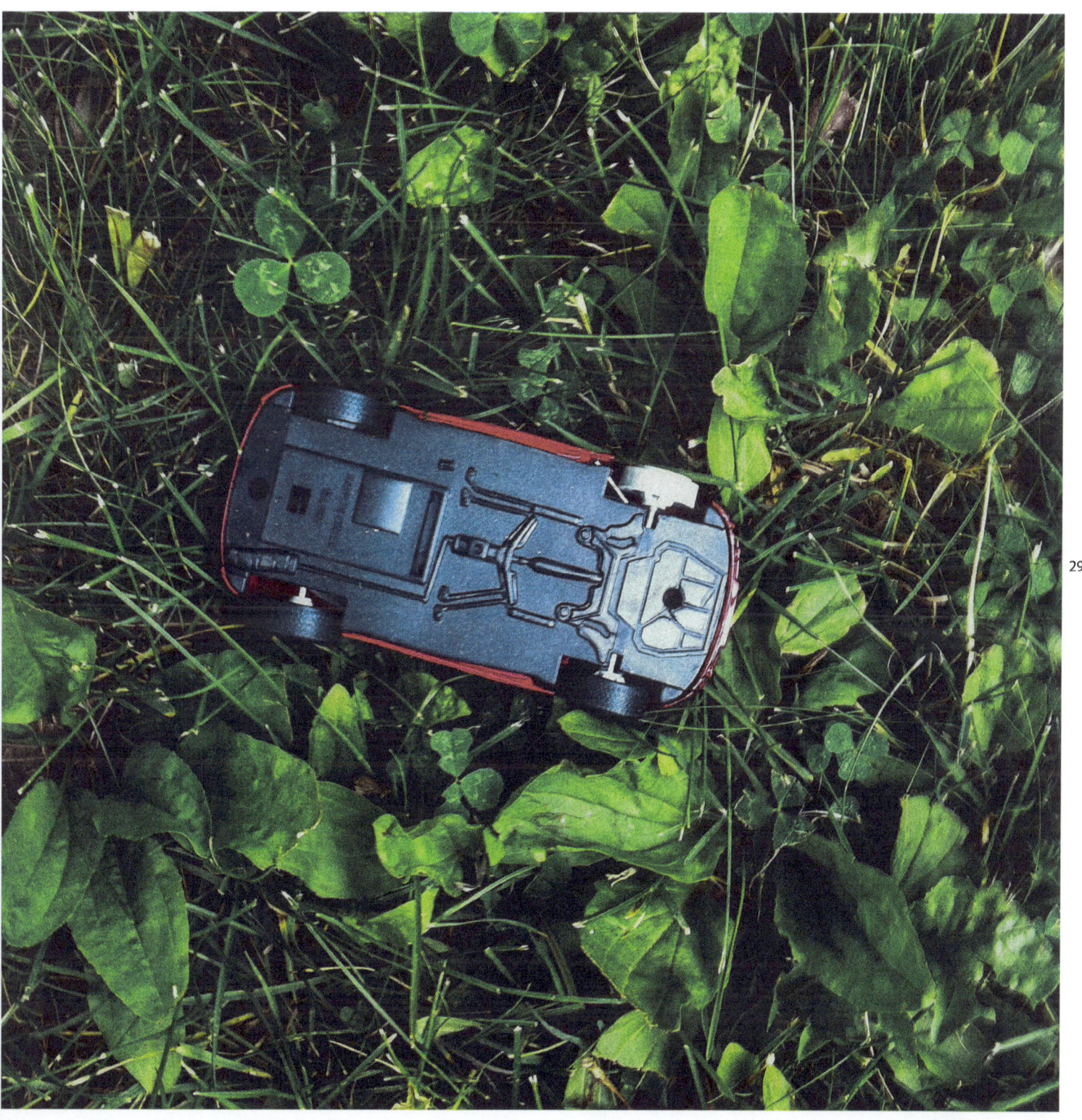

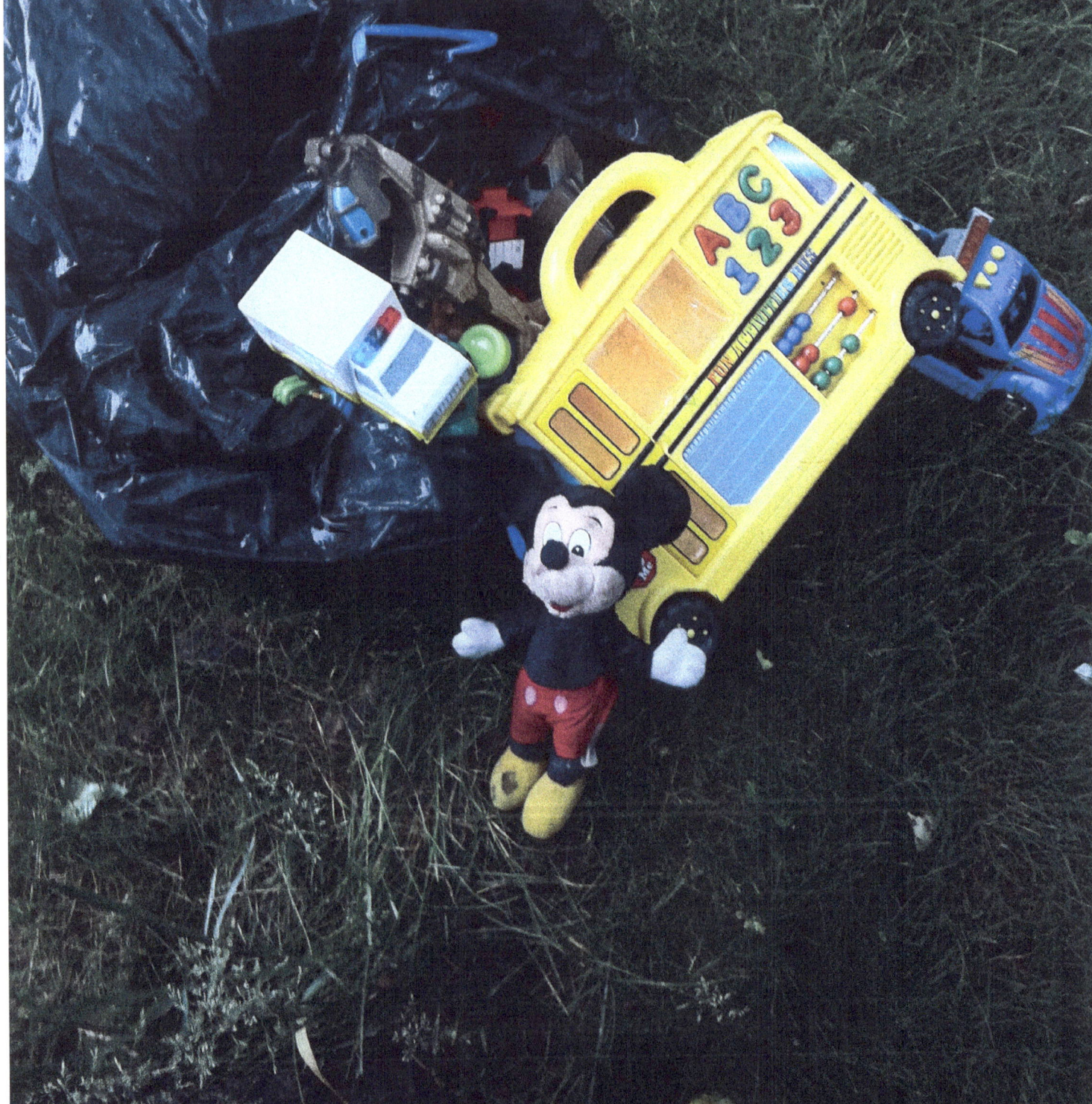

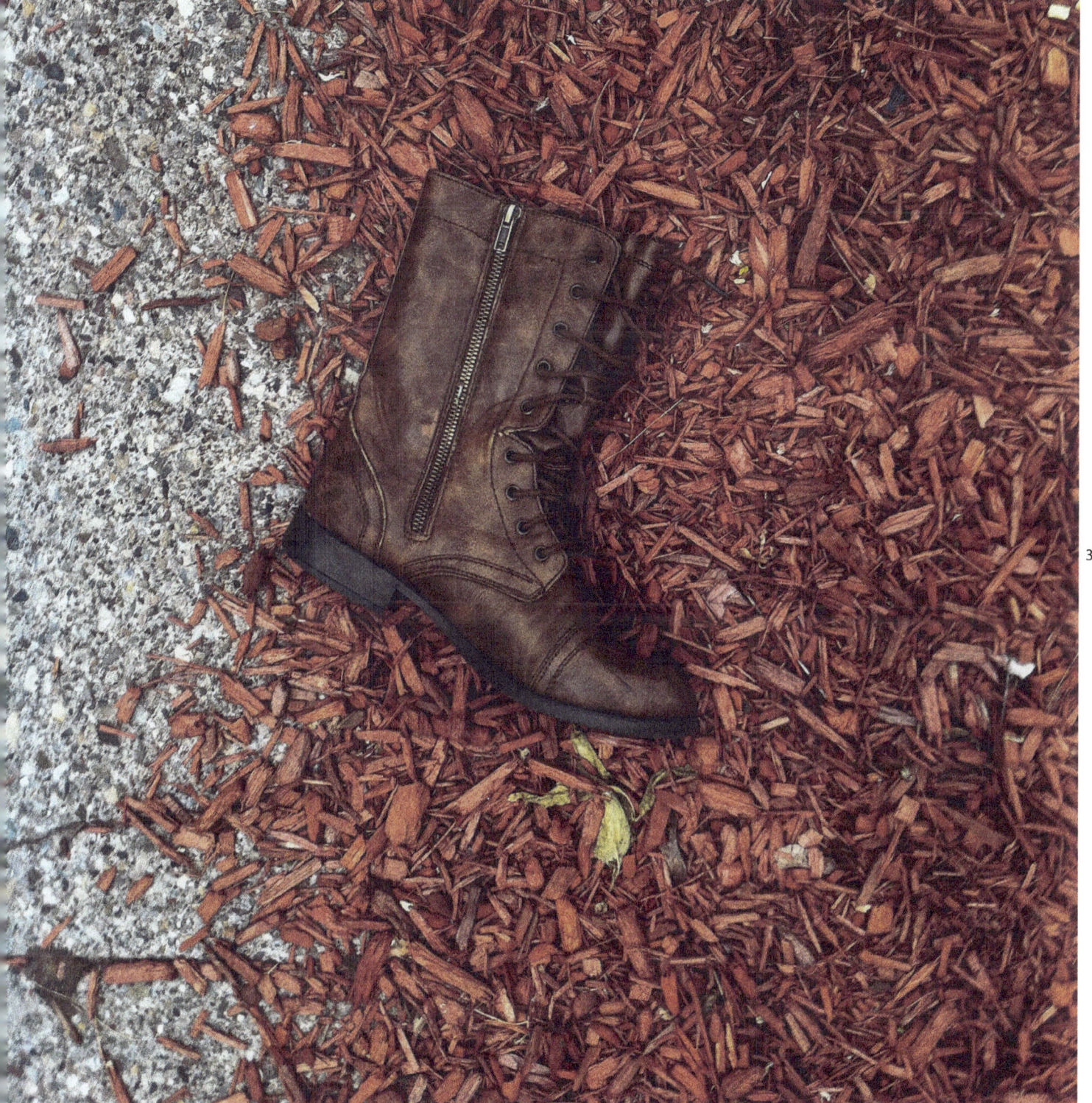

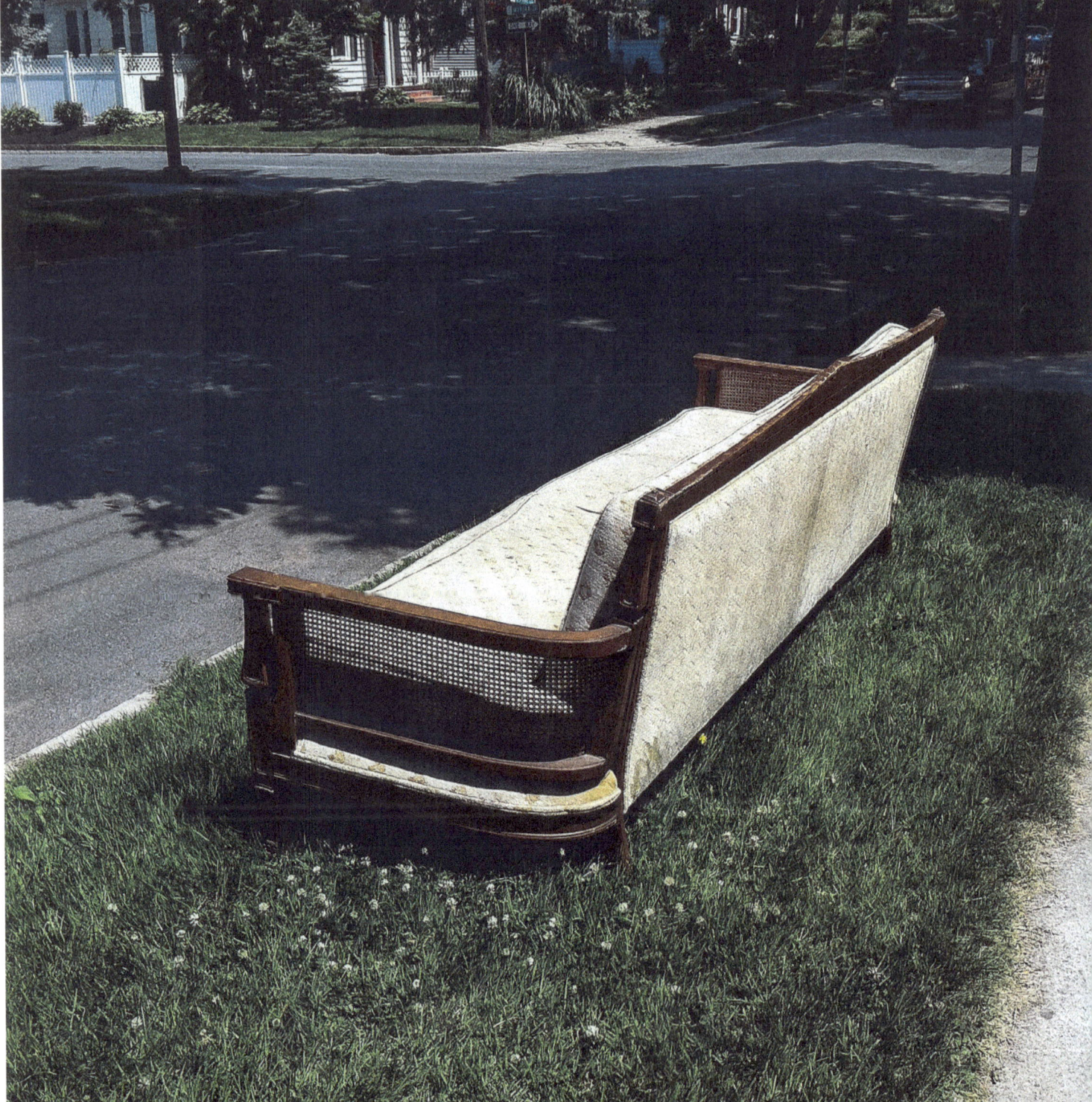

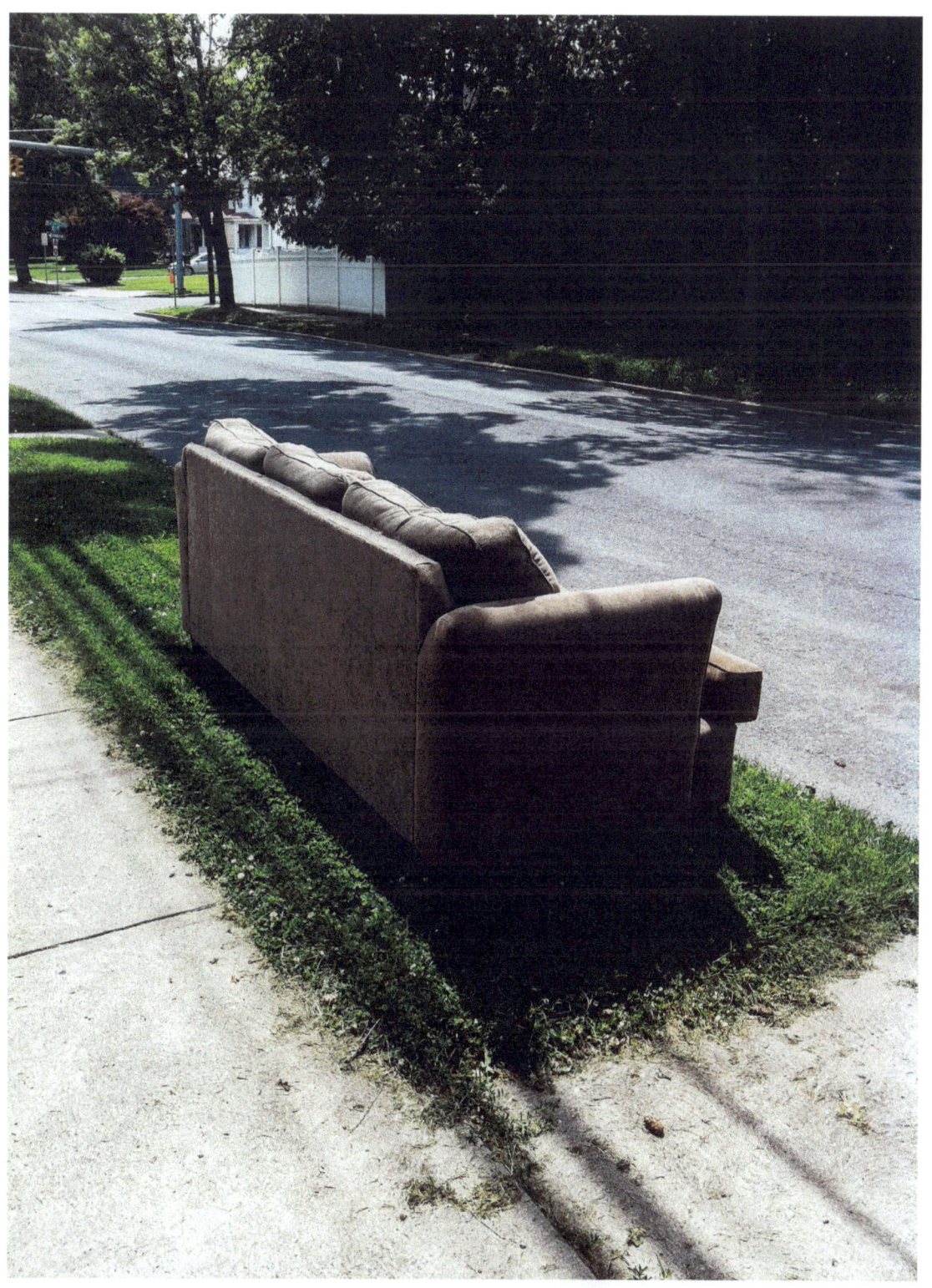

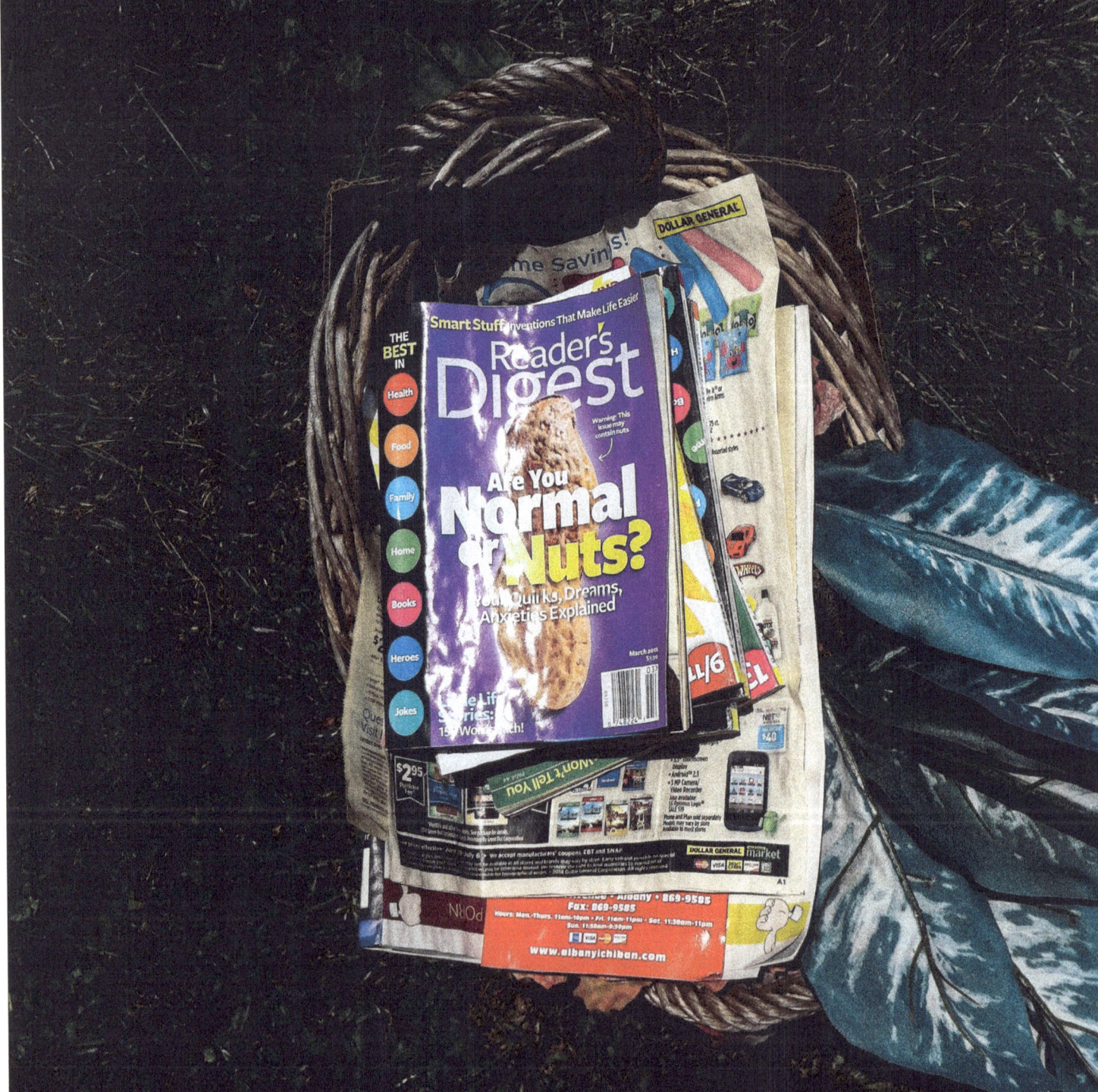

34

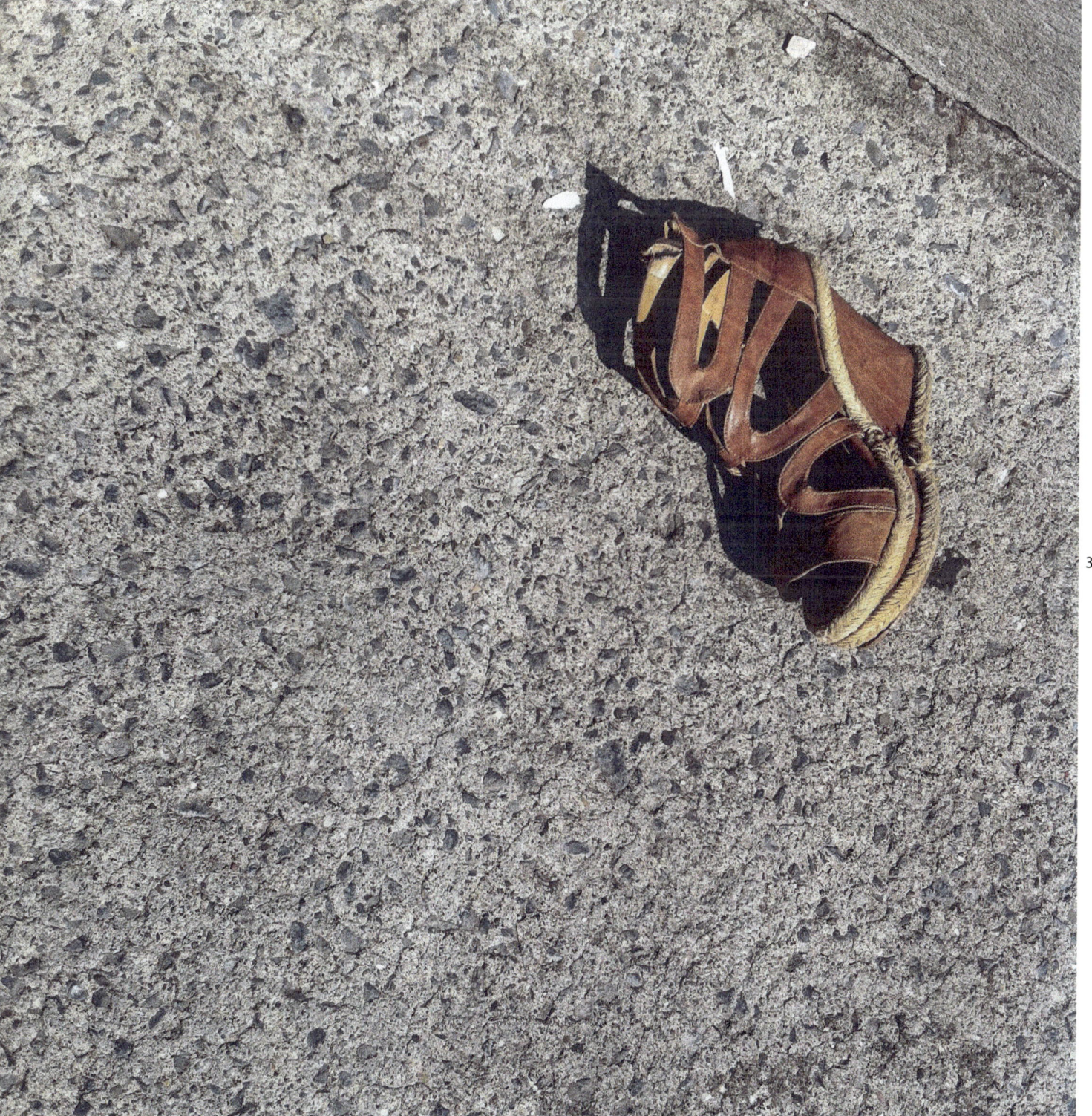

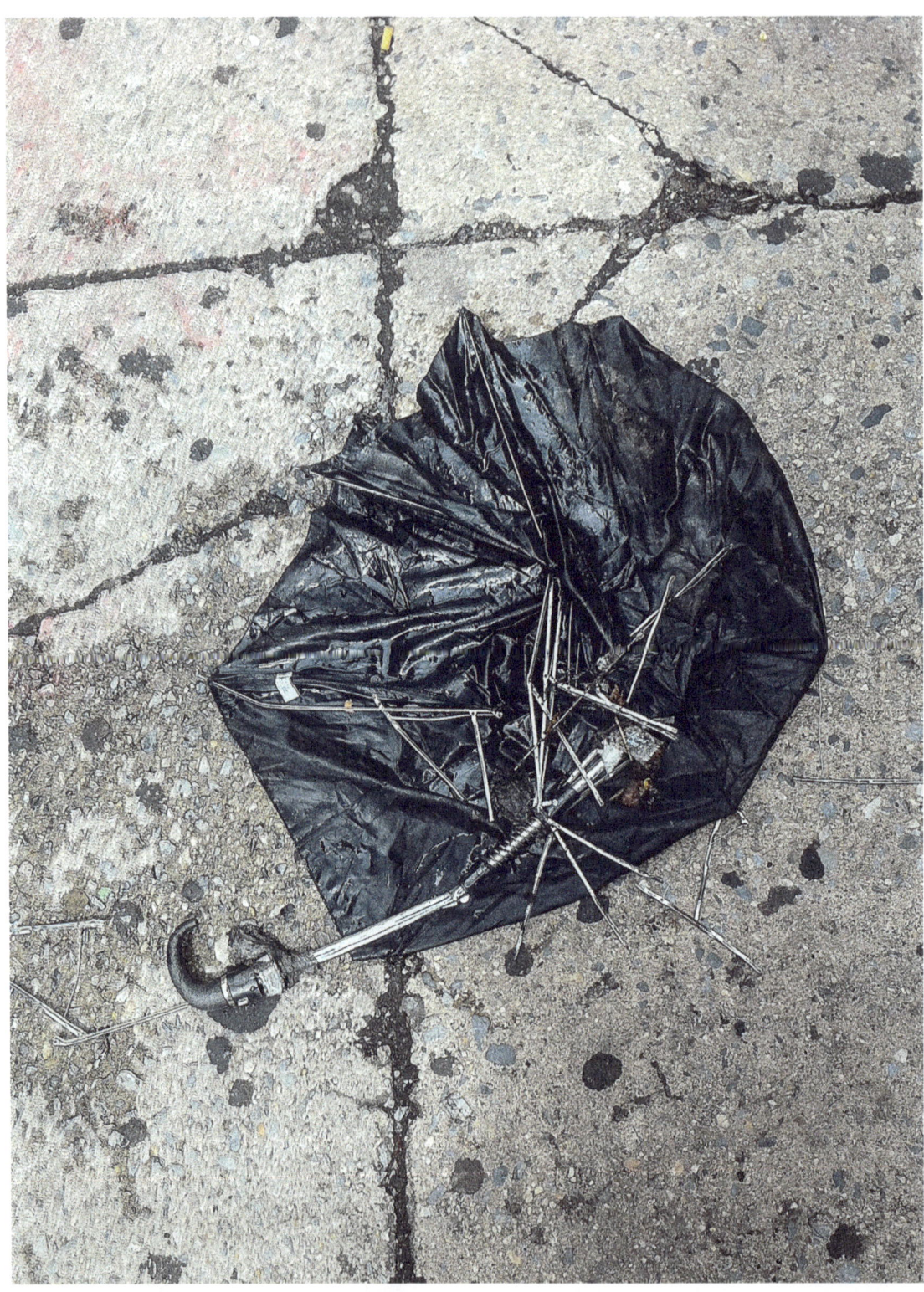

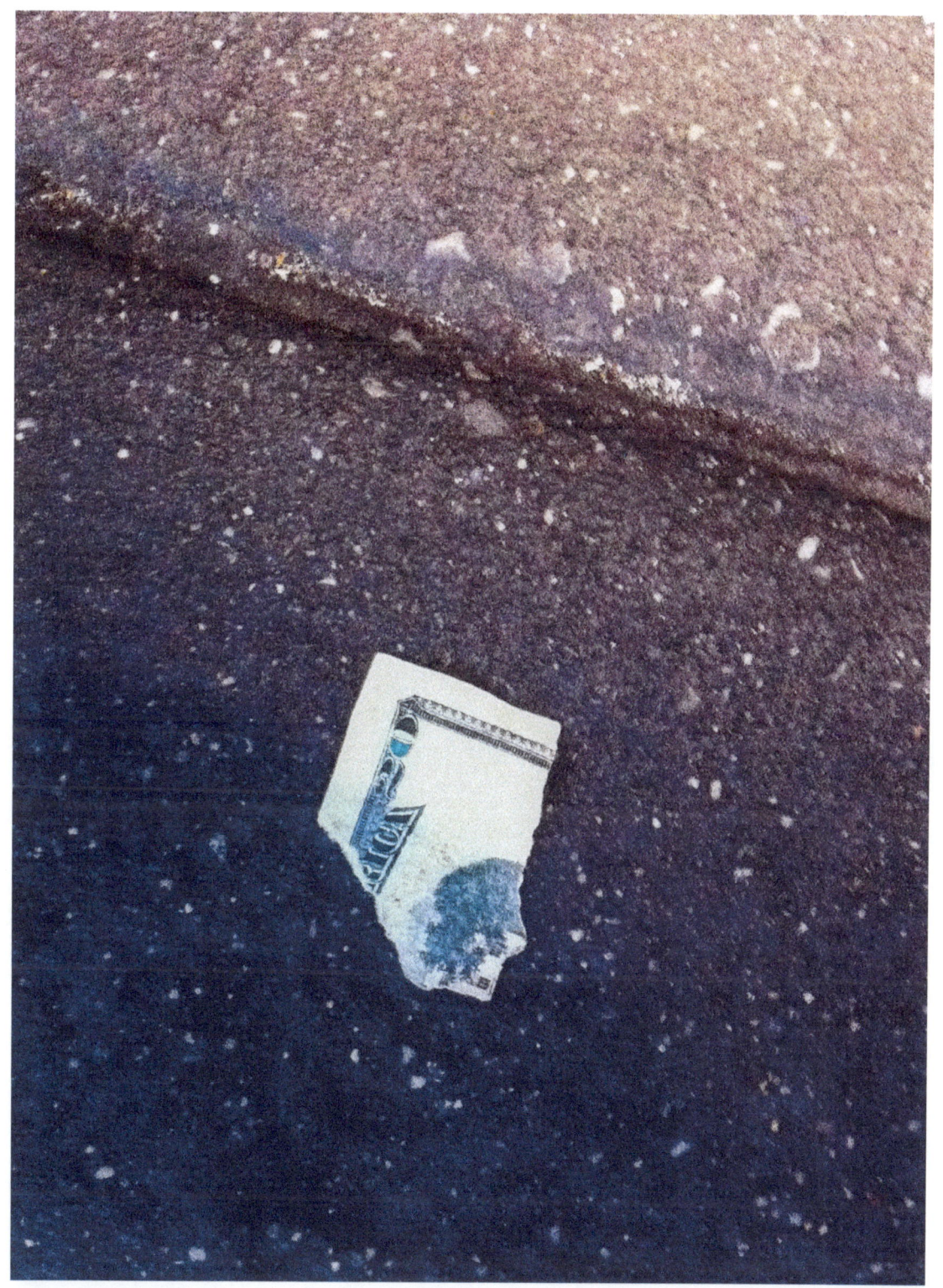

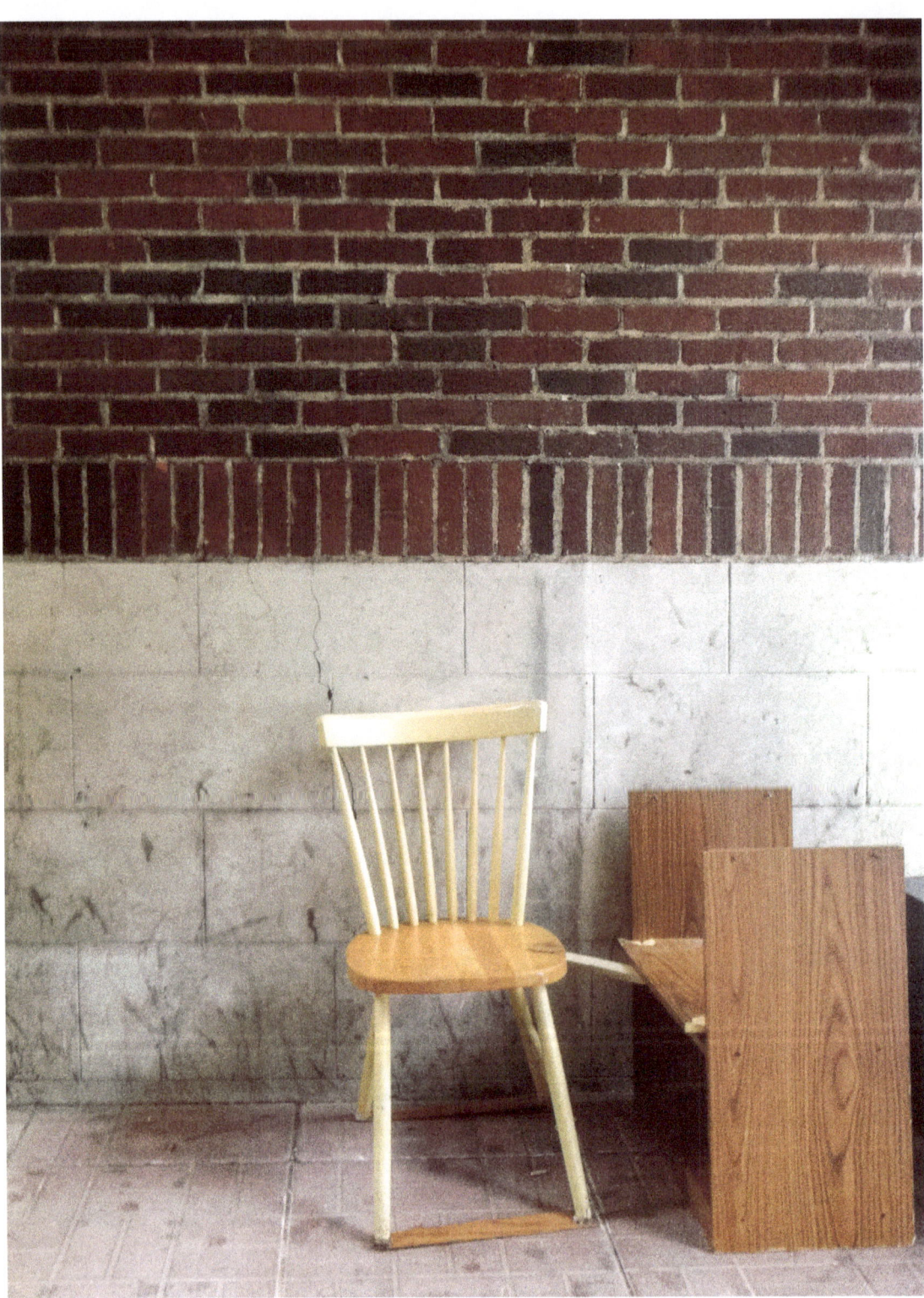

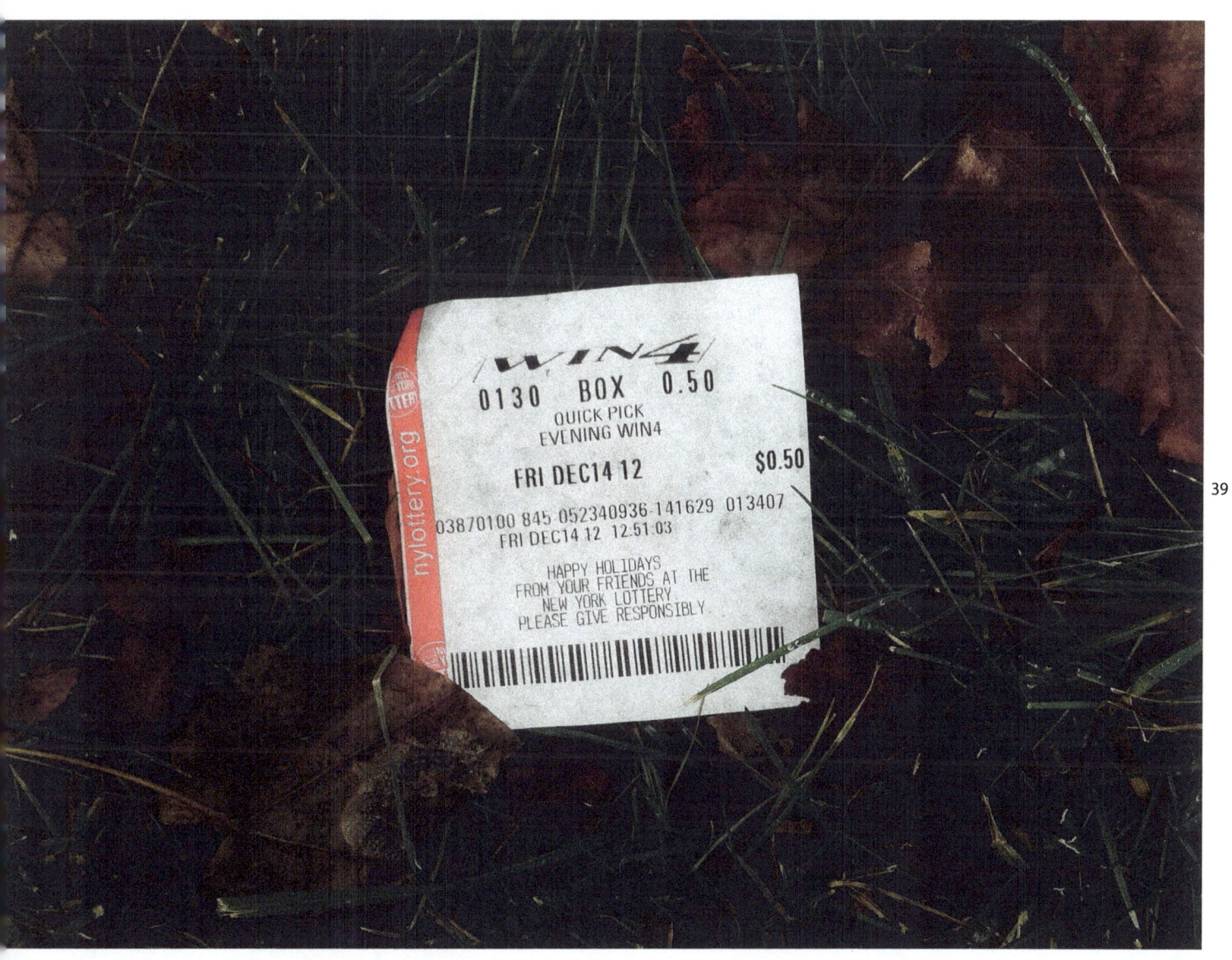

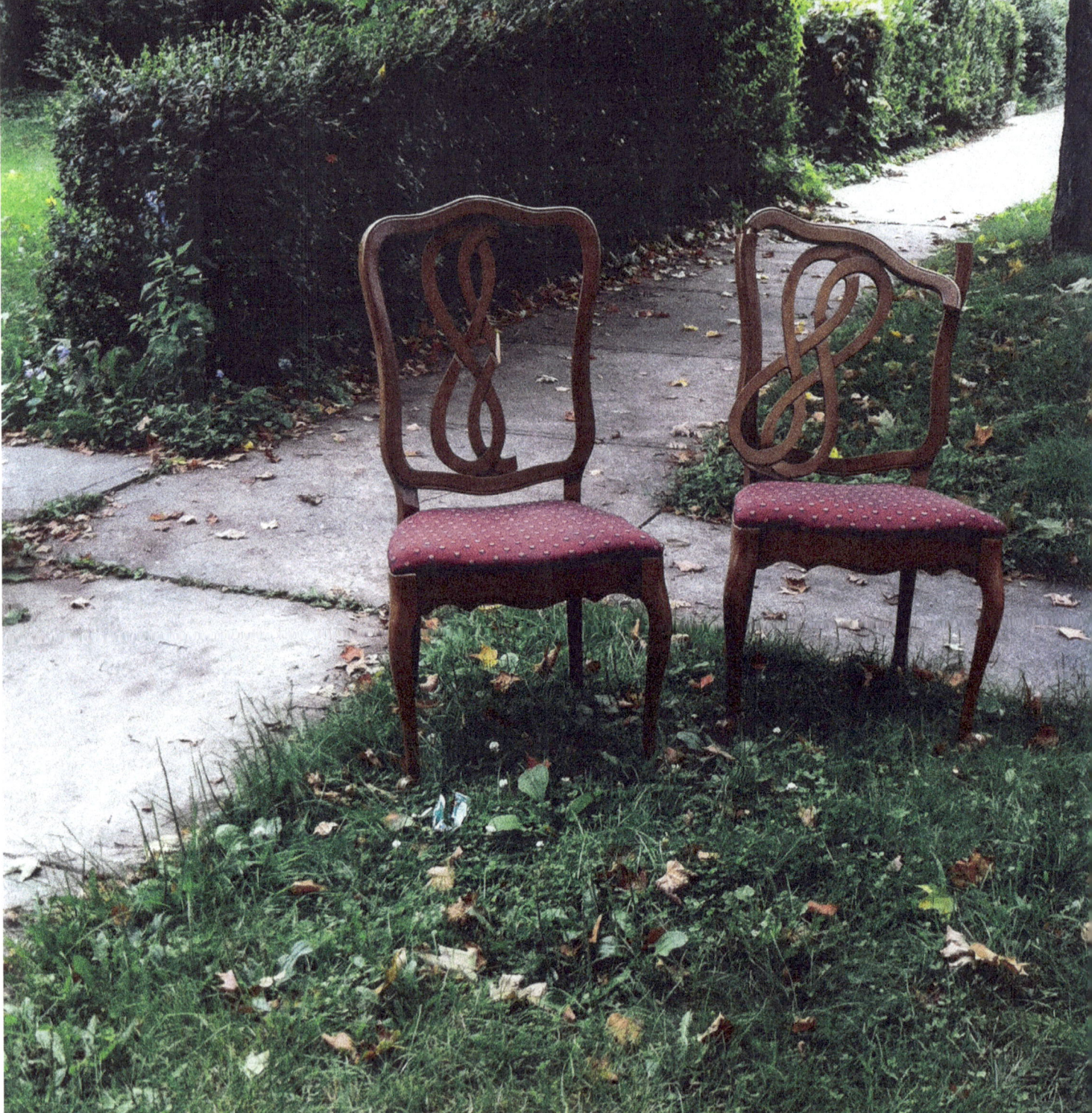

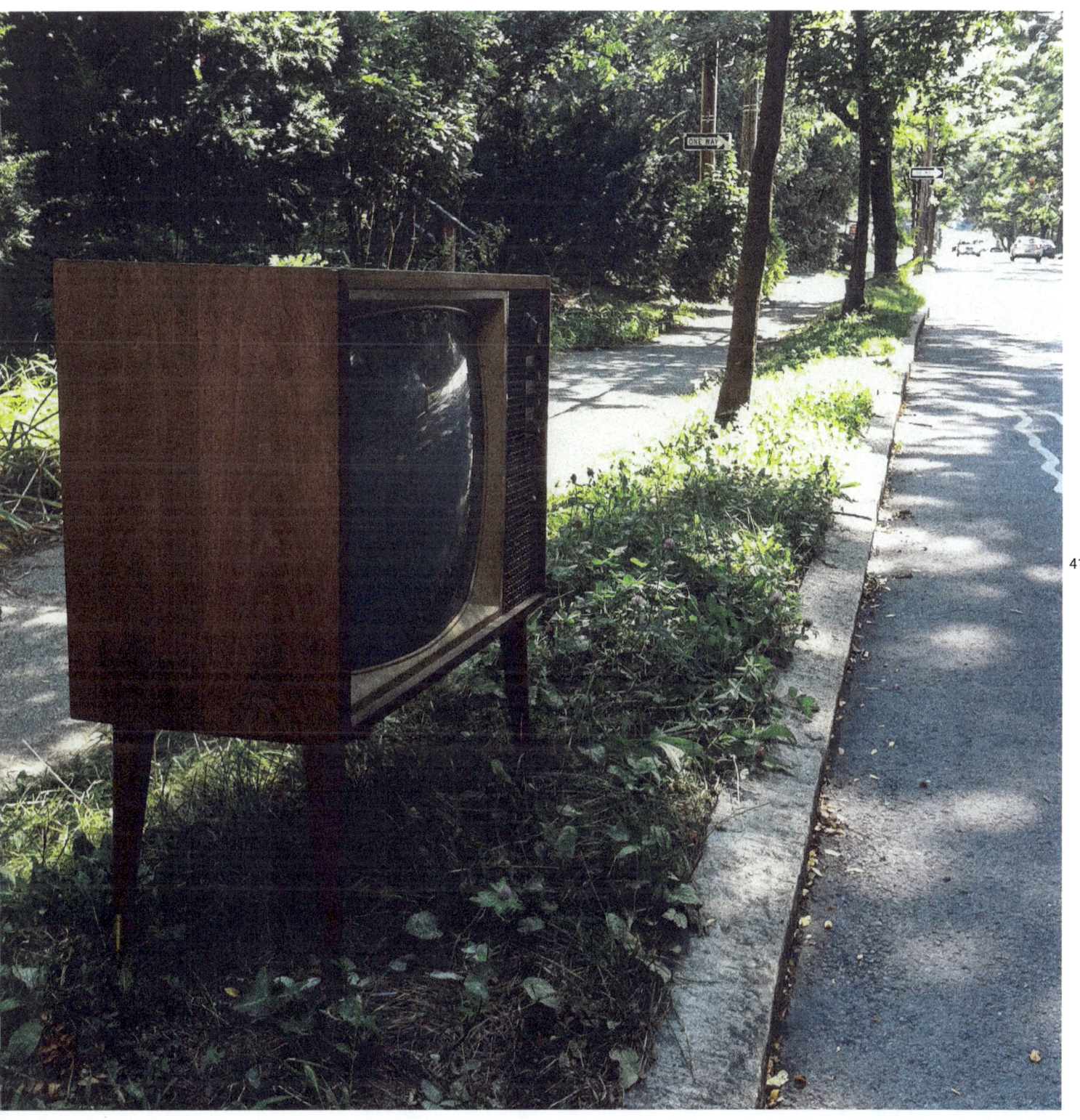

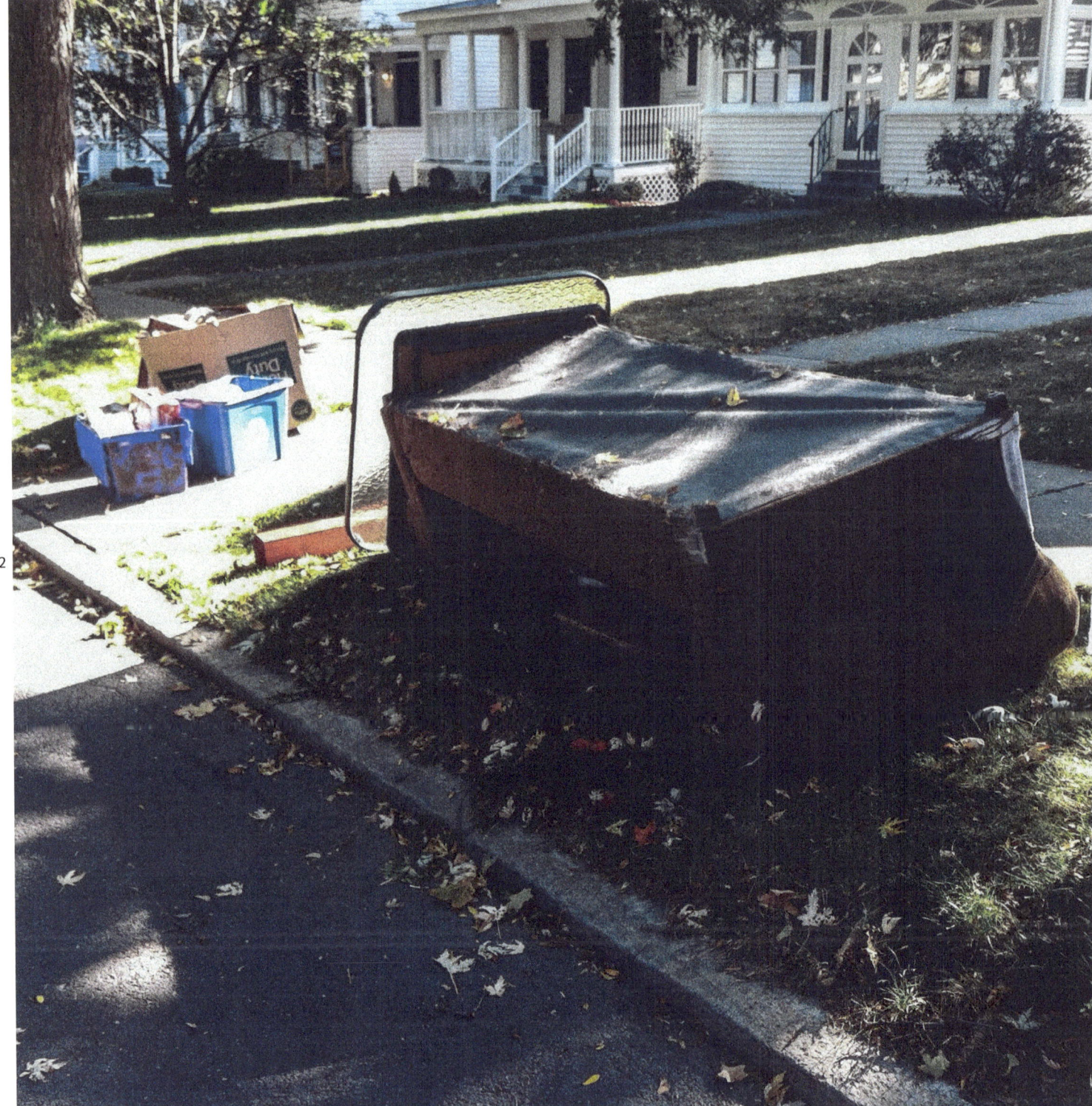

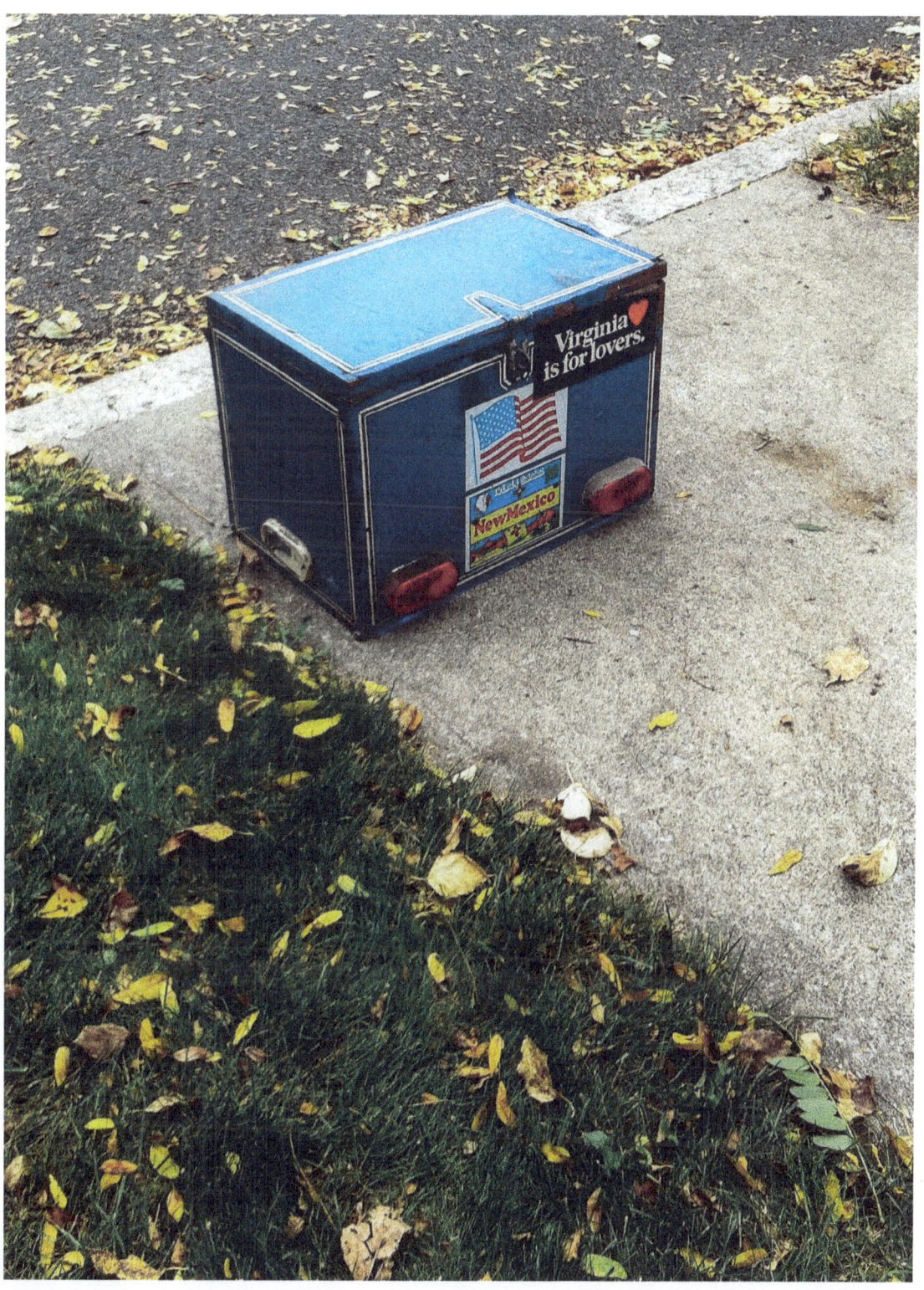

43

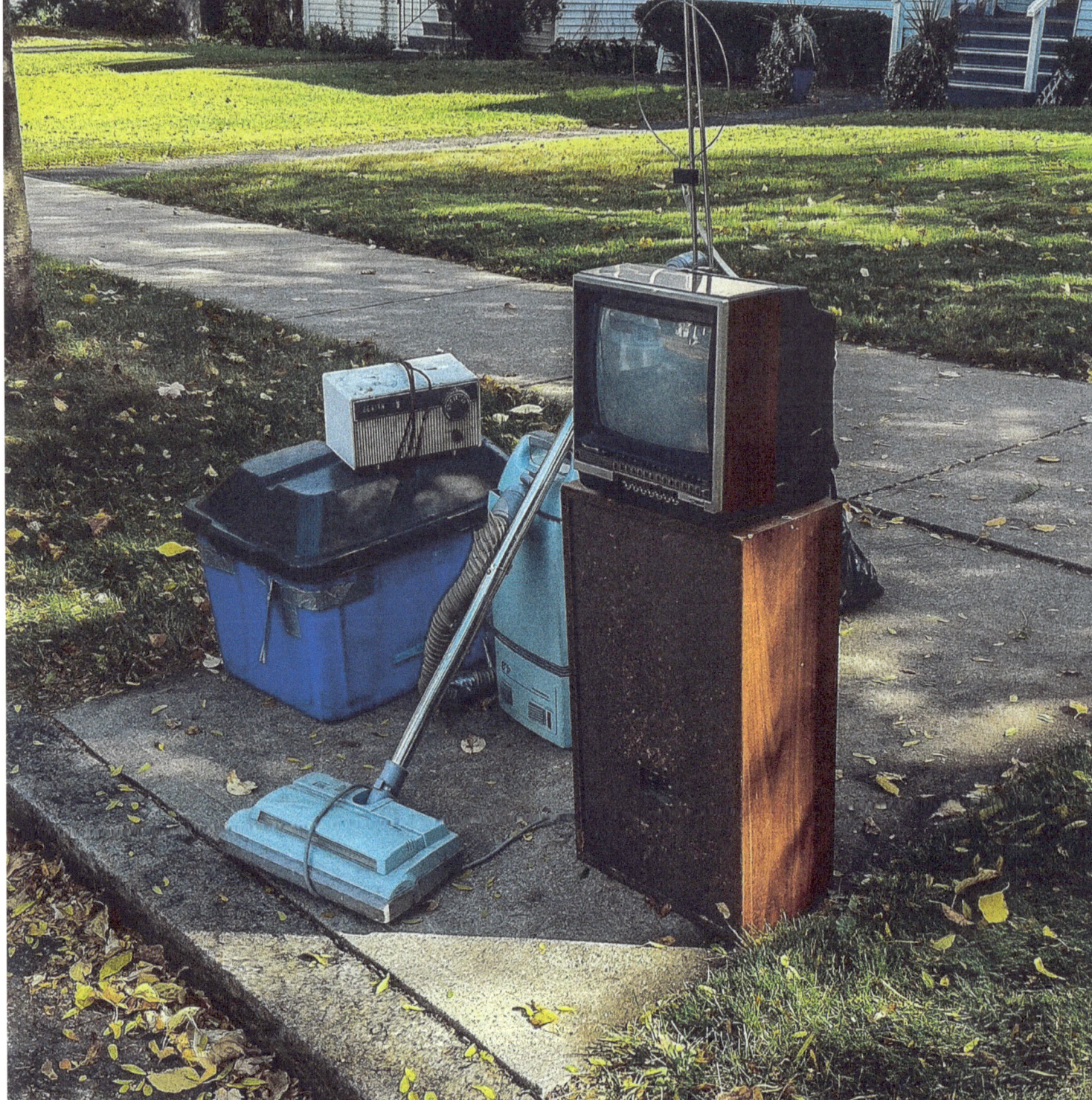

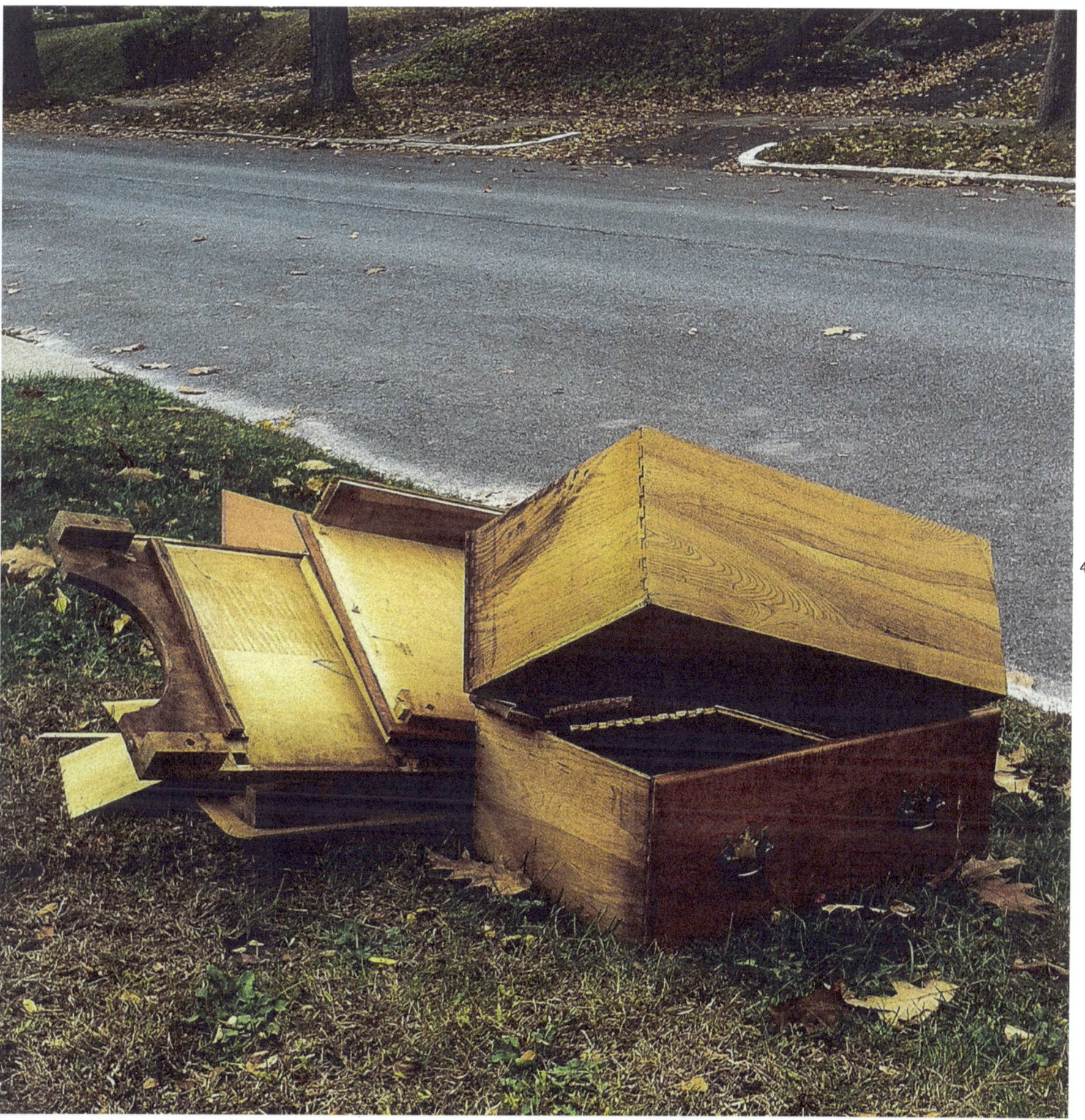

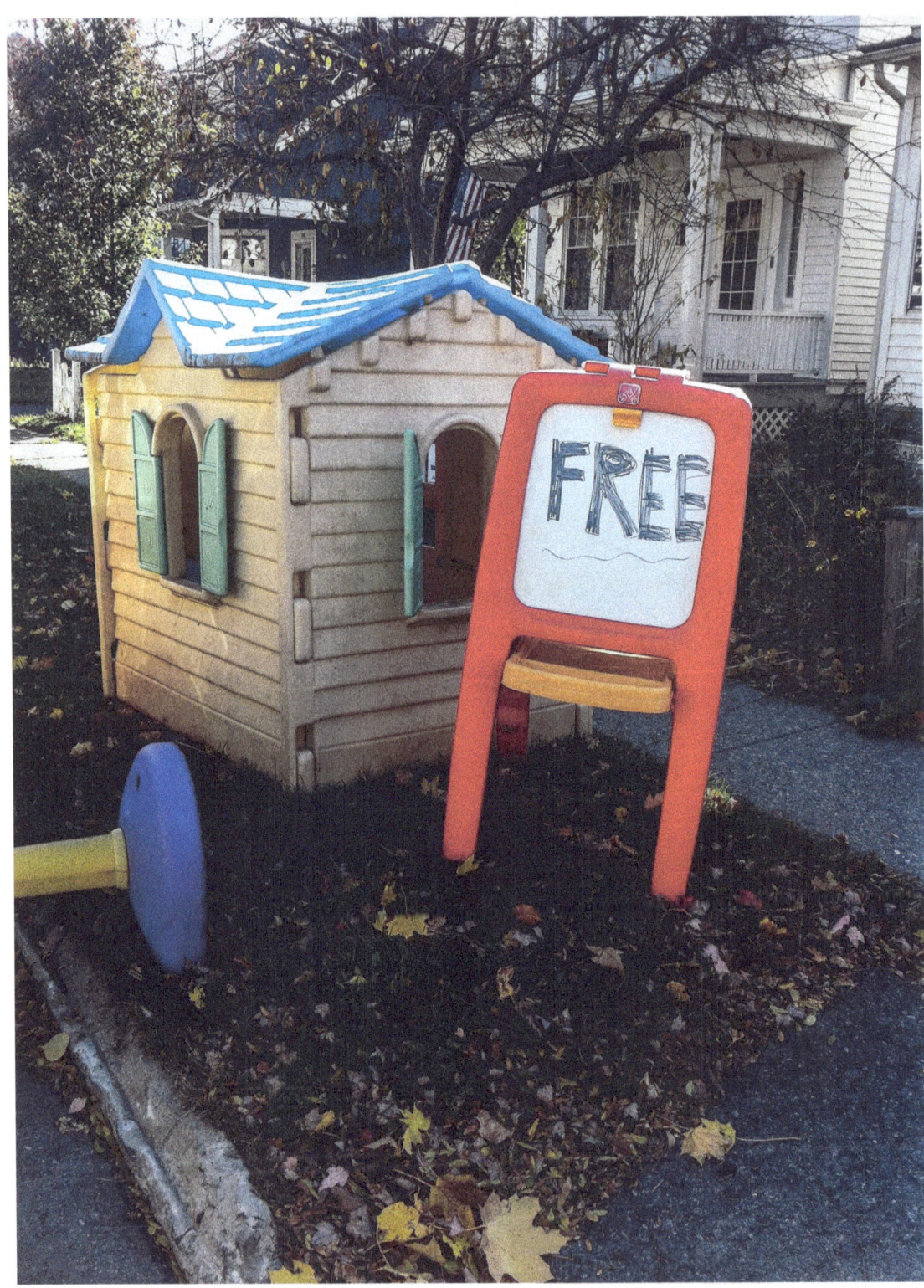

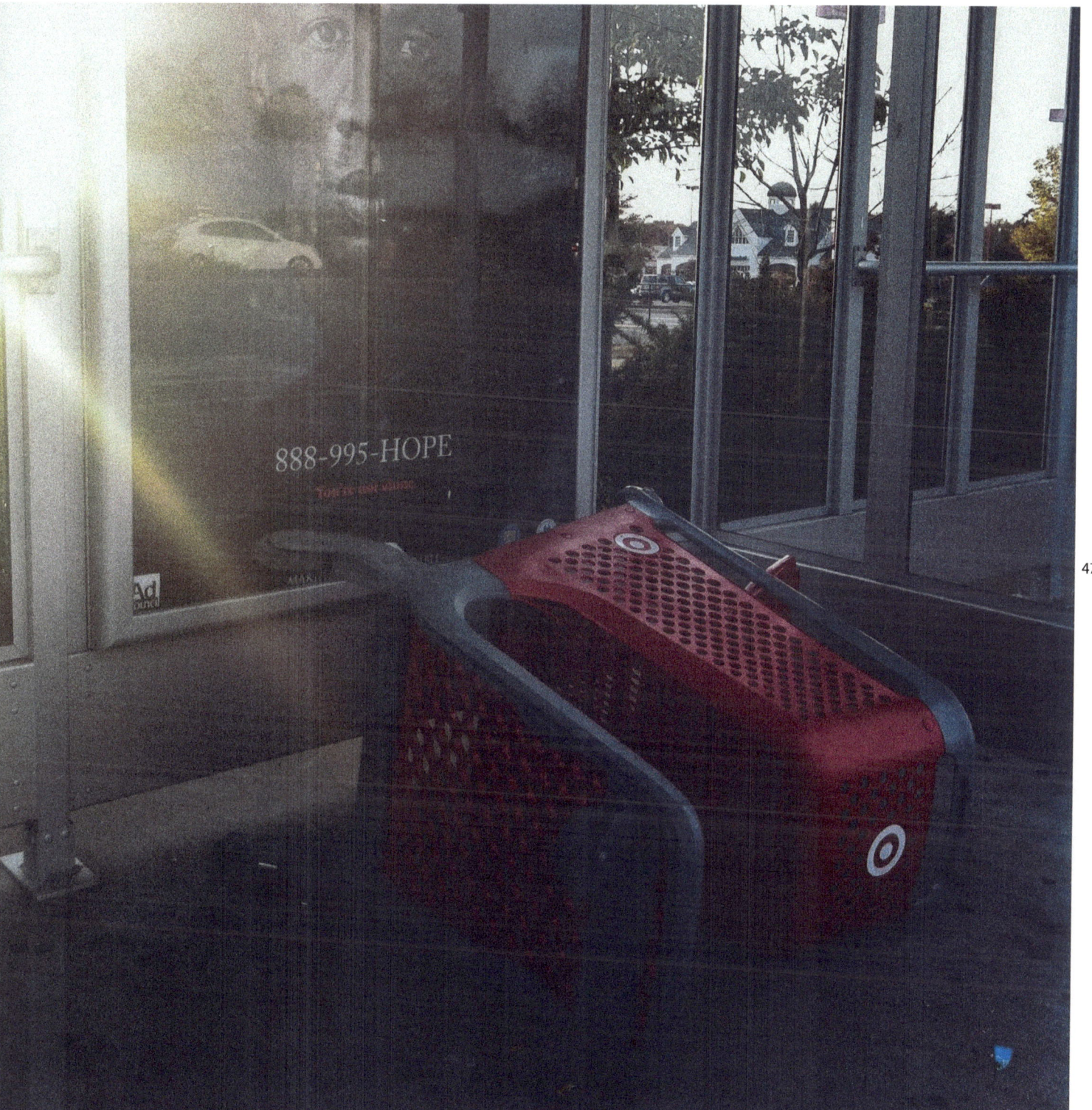

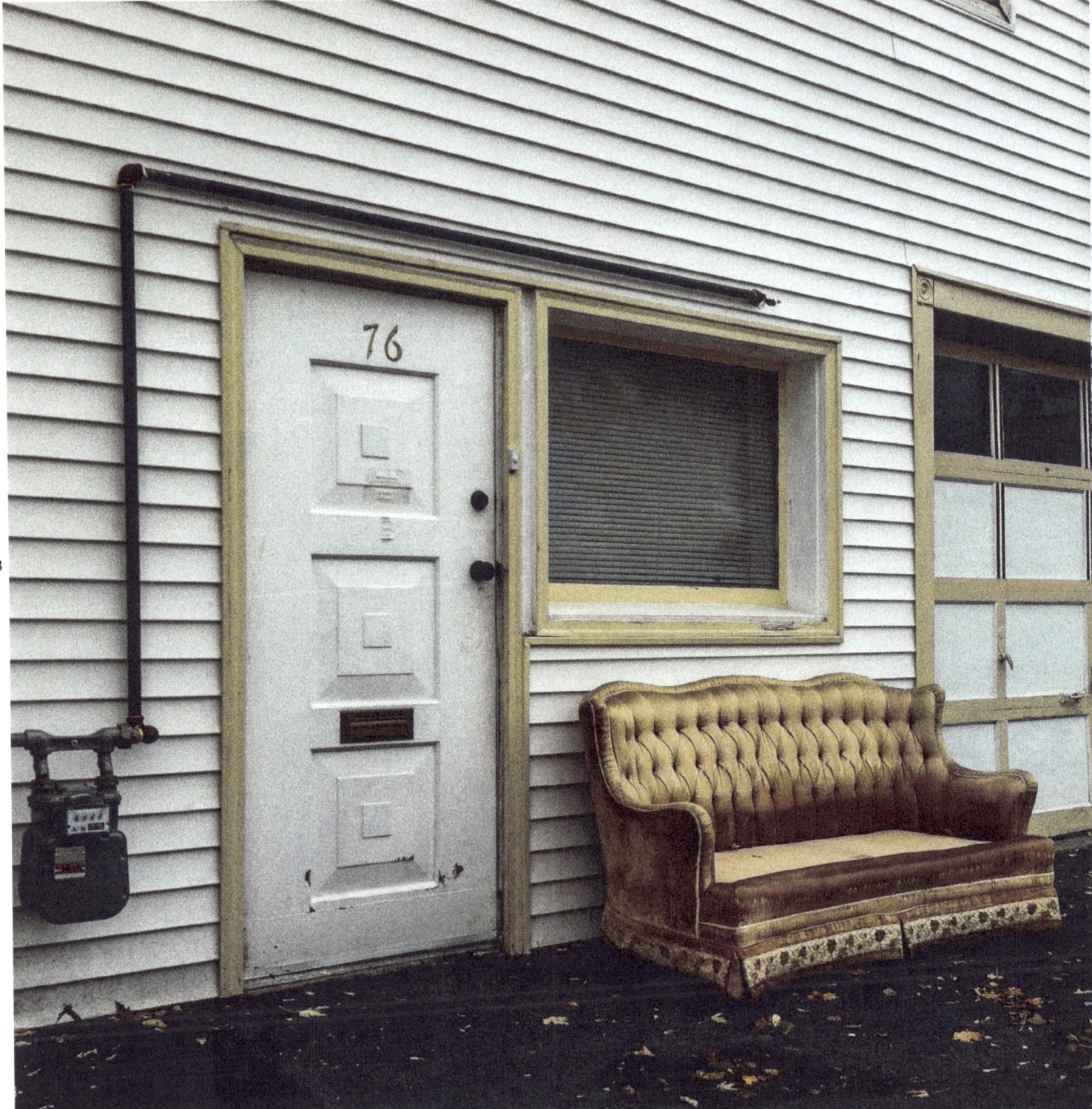

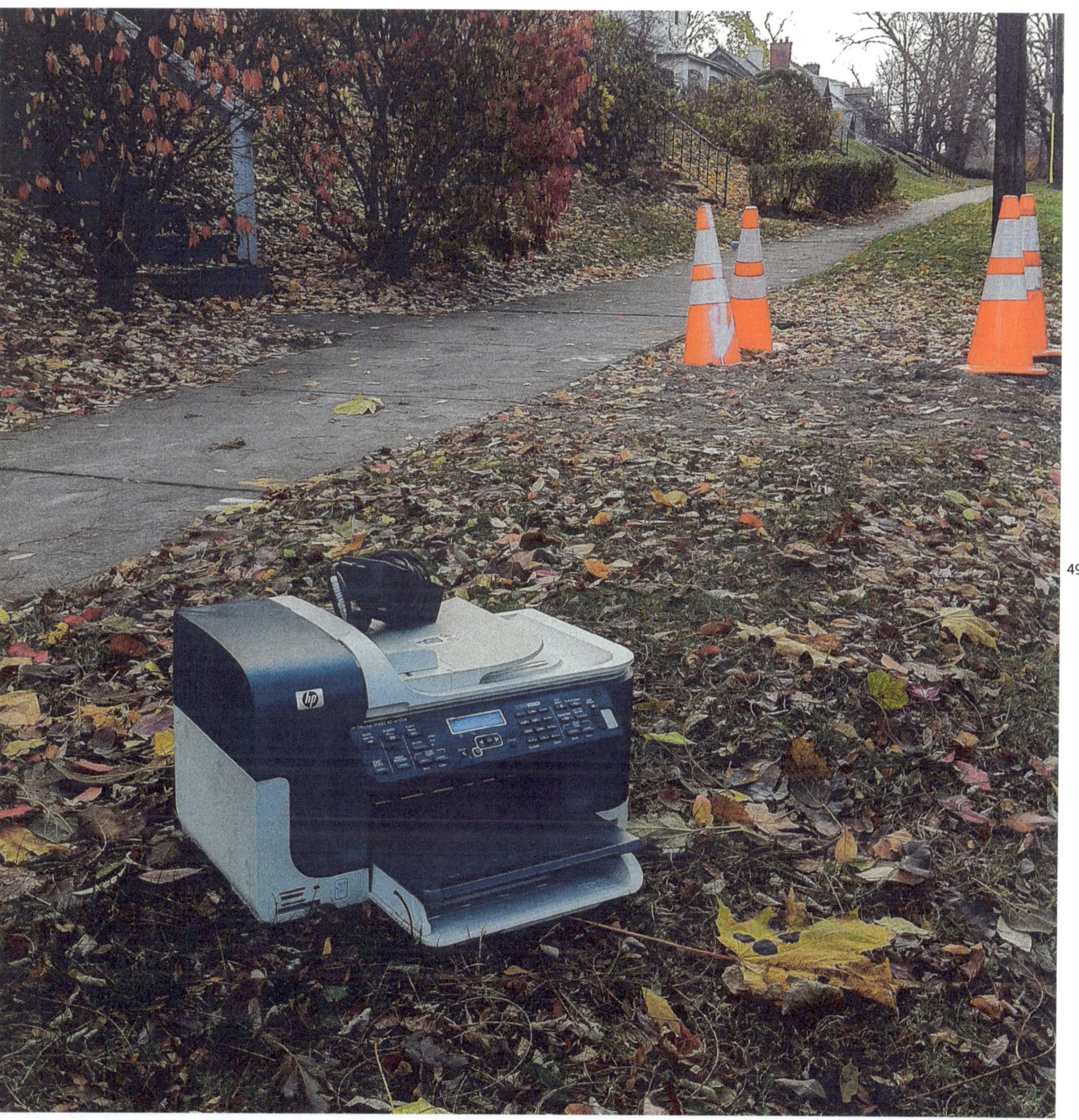

Widarto Adi

Widarto Adi (°1979, Jakarta, Indonesia) makes photos and drawings.
Taking daily life as subject matter, Adi wants to amplify the astonishment
of the spectator by creating compositions or settings that generate
tranquil poetic images that leave traces and balances on the edge of
recognition and alienation.
His works are based on formal associations which open a unique poetic
vein. By applying a poetic and often metaphorical language, he tries to
incite the viewer to make new personal associations.
Widarto Adi currently lives in Albany, New York.